AGAINST THE GRAIN

AN AUTOBIOGRAPHY

BORIS YELTSIN

TRANSLATED BY MICHAEL GLENNY

SUMMIT BOOKS

New York London Toronto Sydney Tokyo Singapore

SUMMIT BOOKS
SIMON & SCHUSTER BUILDING
ROCKEFELLER CENTER
1230 AVENUE OF THE AMERICAS
NEW YORK, NEW YORK 10020

DESIGNED BY EVE METZ
MANUFACTURED IN THE UNITED STATES OF AMERICA

1   3   5   7   9   10   8   6   4   2

ISBN 0-671-70055-3

AUTHOR'S NOTE

Although I have received a number of offers in the past to write my autobiography, I have always declined because of my busy schedule and my feeling that the moment had not yet come for a summing up.

Recent events in the Soviet Union have made me reconsider. Many stormy and dramatic events have taken place during the last year as would, in the past, have taken place over whole decades. We have changed. We have said farewell to an epoch which one would like to believe will never return. There came a time when I realized that perhaps there was, after all, some point in writing about myself and about the recent past through which I have been fated to live.

As I had expected, work on the book had to be done mostly on Sundays and at night, and were it not for the help of the talented young journalist Valentin Yumashev, who fit himself to my working rhythm and devoted a great deal of time to assisting me, it may never have been written.

Devoted assistance, given in a spirit of true friendship, was also provided by Valentina Lantseva, Lev Sukhanov, Tatyana Pushkina—and, of course, my family.

To all of them I give my most heartfelt thanks, and I am grateful to have them by my side.

I wish to donate the earnings from this book to the campaign against AIDS in the Soviet Union. The lack of disposable syringes and other essential instruments in our hospitals has led to a number of cases of children being tragically infected with the disease. I consider it my duty, insofar as I am able, to help fight against this terrible scourge. My royalties will be used to buy disposable syringes and similar necessary equipment. If this is of help to people, I shall be happy.

Boris Yeltsin

EDITOR'S NOTE

The Soviet legislative and political systems may not be familiar to all readers. There is a possibility, too, that further reforms will be enacted before the end of 1990. The following summary offers a brief guide to the offices mentioned in the book.

The Structure of the Soviet Government

Reform of the Soviet government in 1988 led to the creation of the Congress of People's Deputies—2,250 freely elected deputies from throughout the USSR who meet once a year to discuss key legislative issues. The upper chamber of the Congress, known as the Supreme Soviet, is comprised of 542 members elected from the ranks of the Congress and has extensive legislative responsibilities. The Supreme Soviet meets twice a year for three to four months at a time to rule on legislative issues. Made up of two chambers (one with a national focus and one with a regional focus), the Supreme Soviet is headed by a president (currently Mikhail Gorbachev) whose rule is limited to two five-year terms. An elite year-round legislative coordinating body, the Presidium, is made up of executive members from both chambers of the Supreme Soviet.

Administrative matters are dealt with by the government's Council of Ministers, chaired by a prime minister, which oversees the work of the various ministries. The Council of Ministers, unlike the other major government bodies, does not have any legislative function; its purpose is to systemize, execute, and administer the policies of the government.

The Structure of the Communist Party of the Soviet Union

The work of the Soviet government is coordinated and directed by the Communist Party of the Soviet Union (CPSU), the only political party allowed in the USSR. At the local level, party officials serve as secretaries of their district, city, province, or region, addressing matters of significance to their constituents. At the national level, delegates from party organizations all over the country form the Communist Party Congress, which meets at least once every five years and elects the Central Committee from its members. The Central Committee meets at least twice a year to draft policy proposals that are passed on to the Politburo, an elite body whose members are elected from and by the Central Committee.

The Politburo consists of approximately twenty members (not all of whom have voting privileges) who formulate party policy at full general assemblies (plenums). The Politburo is the center of executive power in the Soviet Union; its decrees are forwarded to the Supreme Soviet for enactment into law. The Central Committee and Politburo are supported by an extensive permanent staff of career bureaucrats known as the *apparat*, whose senior members make up the Secretariat. Heading the entire CPSU organization is the General Secretary of the Communist Party (currently Mikhail Gorbachev), who often serves as president of the Supreme Soviet as well.

AGAINST
THE
GRAIN

Prologue

Chronicle of the Election Campaign

There would seem to be no more room for doubt. The election of people's deputies takes place tomorrow, and in the Moscow number 1 constituency, where the candidates are Yuri Brakov and myself, the Muscovites (and there are six million of them in this constituency) should elect me as their deputy by an overwhelming majority. All the official and unofficial public opinion polls, including the American predictions, say so; this is confirmed by the preelection mood, and my intuition simply tells me that all will be well.

For some reason, though, I still can't sleep. Once again I

13

run through all the events that have befallen me during recent months, weeks, and days. I try to understand where I made mistakes and where I did the right thing. Mistakes there were, and I am grateful for them; they spurred me on, made me work with twice, three times my usual energy. When analyzing situations and events, I ignore whatever went well and concentrate on my shortcomings and errors. This is a basic trait of my character; I don't know whether it is good or bad. But it accounts for my feeling of permanent dissatisfaction with myself, a dissatisfaction with 90 percent of what I do.

Tomorrow's election will be a summing-up of the past eighteen months of my life, in which I have been both a political pariah and a holder of several resounding party appointments. I have been out of politics since I resigned from the Politburo in 1987. In Stalin's time, ex-politicians were shot; Khrushchev pensioned them off; in Brezhnev's "era of stagnation," they were packed off as ambassadors to distant countries. Here, too, Gorbachev's *perestroika* has set a new precedent: A dismissed politician is now given the opportunity of returning to political life.

It was Gorbachev himself who telephoned me after my resignation from the Politburo. He offered me the post of first deputy chairman of the State Committee for Construction (Gosstroi). I accepted it, since at that moment I was indifferent to what my next job might be. At the end of our conversation, he told me to bear in mind that he wasn't going to let me back into politics. At the time, he evidently believed with all sincerity in what he was saying; it did not occur to him that he had created and put in motion a set of democratic processes under which his word as general secretary ceased to be the word of a dictator—a word that, in the past, had been immediately transformed into law, binding on the whole empire. Now the general secretary of the Central Committee of the Communist Party, the heart of the Soviet government, might say that he was not going to let me back into politics, but the people might think otherwise and decide that I must be allowed back. And now they can do this: Times have certainly changed.

And the people will bring us much more that is new! That is one delightful aspect of the present time. But it is also a time fraught with trouble. Nobody knows what will happen next, or where the step we have taken today may lead us tomorrow. The apparat, the huge, lumbering machine of the party bureaucracy, is making clumsy maneuvers in its defensive attempts at self-preservation, but by so doing it will surely destroy itself all the sooner. In my case, it was given a limited and not particularly complicated task to perform—mainly to make sure that I was not elected as a people's deputy. After all, it should not have been a difficult assignment to carry out. It was nothing compared with providing a flat for every Soviet family by the year 2000 or ensuring that the country is decently fed within the current five-year plan. All they had to do was deal with one person! What's more, they would be aided by a remarkable new electoral law, with its nominating meetings carefully designed to sift out undesirable candidates; by the excessive powers given to the constituency commissions (all designed by the party bureaucrats themselves); and by control over a vast, obedient propaganda machine, which would say and publish just what they wanted! Yet with all this available to them, they still managed to fail. All the dirty tricks they used against me in the past months—juggling the facts, telling lies, making stern denunciations of me at the full legislative assembly meeting (plenum) of the Central Committee—have had exactly the opposite effect to that intended and have only brought me the ever greater support of the electorate.

Each time a new piece of stupidity was aimed at me, invariably evoking a surge of sympathy for me from the voters of Moscow, I became more acutely aware of what a morass we have sunk into and how immeasurably difficult it is going to be to haul ourselves out of it. For it is precisely these people —the party bureaucracy—who are doing their best to put new obstacles in the way of *perestroika* and *glasnost*. And they are not prepared to surrender their right to do so. It is at such moments of insight that it is easiest to throw up one's hands in despair. Thanks, however, to the fact that during the election campaign I was able to meet my electors almost every day, I drew new energy from them and a renewed faith that we will never again live as we lived before. The era of moral slavery is over.

But what if I am the loser in tomorrow's election? What will that mean? That the party bureaucracy was after all the stronger, that injustice has triumphed? Nothing of the sort. Simply that I, too, am human and that I have many failings. I have an awkward, obstinate character; I have made misjudgments and mistakes, so that it is entirely possible that I may not be elected. But even if the vote goes to Brakov—which is what the party bureaucrats are counting on—it is a profound illusion to imagine that he will become the obedient tool of those who put him up to it. In today's climate, both he and I —or anyone else—can fulfill the role of people's deputy only by listening to the people and not to the bureaucracy, by carrying out the demands of the people and not of the party's establishment.

And yet I believe that the people of Moscow will vote for me. There is not long to wait now.

1

December 13, 1988

Chronicle of the Election Campaign

Right or wrong, I have made a decision: I will run for office in the election of people's deputies. I fully realize that my prospects of being elected are far from being 100 percent, as the new electoral law enables the government and the party apparat to control much of the proceedings. There are several hurdles to be overcome before the voters make their choice. The system of proposing candidates; the nominating meetings to sift out the unsuitable ones; the elector commissions, which are packed with apparatchiks, the bureaucrats of the local party executive committee—all this gives rise to gloomy

17

reflection. If I lose, if I fail to be elected, I can only imagine the triumph and delight with which the party establishment will rush to give me the coup de grace. It would be their trump card: The people didn't want him, the people didn't put him forward as a candidate, the people threw him out. But in reality, the nominating meetings have no connection whatsoever with the expression of the people's will. This is obvious to everyone, from the rank-and-file voter all the way to Gorbachev himself. It is simply a support to prop up a collapsing system of government, a bone thrown to the party's bureaucratic apparat.

It would be perfectly possible not to stand for election; close friends have advised me to keep out of this fight, because the odds are stacked against me. For the last eighteen months the very name Yeltsin has been under a ban; I was alive, but it was as if I didn't exist. So if I suddenly reemerge into the political arena and start talking to the voters and taking part in rallies and meetings, then the whole of the party's immensely powerful propaganda machine will come down on me with a barrage of lies, slander, and half-truths.

Furthermore, under the new electoral system, ministers, the position I hold now, do not have the right to be people's deputies. Consequently, if I am elected I will have to resign from my ministerial post. After that, who knows what may happen? The Congress of People's Deputies, elected under the present system, is more than likely to see to it that I am not elected to the Supreme Soviet of the USSR, and I shall therefore be unable to work in the parliament. So, if I lose, I am faced with the more than real prospect of becoming, at best, an unemployed deputy. As far as I know, not a single minister intends to give up his job. There are a lot of people's deputies but few ministers.

Telegrams have started to come in from all over the country. Huge organizations, many of them several thousand strong, have been putting me forward as their candidate.

They come from so far and wide that one can learn the geography of the Soviet Union from them.

I know that the election is going to be a battle, exhausting and nerve-racking. What's more, my enemies will bend the rules and hit below the belt; they will attack me suddenly from behind and use all sorts of illegal but nevertheless effective methods. Knowing all this, I question whether I am prepared to endure the long, hard election campaign.

As I debate the matter to myself, I have many doubts. I almost persuade myself not to run. But most interesting of all is that inwardly I have long ago made the decision—perhaps it happened at the very moment when I learned that these elections were now going to be possible. Yes, of course, I am going to throw myself into this crazy maelstrom, and it is entirely possible that this time I shall break my neck, but I cannot do otherwise.

When did you start to become a rebel?

Whom do you most resemble in character—your mother or your father?

Tell us about your parents in a little more detail.

It's said that you used to be a real sportsman and you even played on a championship team. Is that a rumor, or is it true?*

I was born on February 1, 1931, in the village of Butko in the Talitsky district of Sverdlovsk province, where all my forebears had lived. They had plowed the land, sown wheat, and passed their lives like all other country people. Among the

* Questions from the floor at meetings during the election campaign.

21

people in our village there were the Yeltsins, my father's family, and the Starygins, my mother's family. My father married my mother there, and soon I made my appearance in the world—their first child.

My mother used to tell me the story of what happened at my baptism. The little church, with its priest, was the only one for the whole district, which consisted of several villages. The birth rate for the area was quite high, but even so the baptismal service was held only once a month. Consequently, that day was a busy one for the priest, and the church was filled to bursting with parents, babies, relatives, and friends. The baptism was conducted in the most primitive fashion: There was a tub full of holy liquid, water seasoned with something or other, in which each baby was completely immersed. The squalling infant was then christened and given a name, which was entered in the parish register. And of course, as was the custom in villages all over Russia, the parents offered the priest a glass of home-brewed beer, moonshine, or vodka —whatever they could afford.

Since my turn did not come until the afternoon, the priest, having drunk many toasts, could barely stand. When my mother, Klavdia Vasilievna, and my father, Nikolai Ignatievich, handed me to him, the priest dropped me into the tub and, being drawn into an argument with a member of the congregation, forgot to take me out. At first, my parents, who were standing at some distance from the baptismal font, didn't know what had happened. When they finally realized what was going on, my mother screamed, leapt forward, and fished me out from somewhere at the bottom of the tub.

They then shook the water out of me. The priest was not particularly worried. He said, "Well, if he can survive such an ordeal, it means he's a good, tough lad—and I name him Boris."

Thus I became Boris Nikolayevich. I won't say that after that I developed any special affinity for religion; of course not.

22

My childhood was passed during hard times: very bad harvests and no food. We were all forced to join a collective farm —and all of us were treated like peasants. To make matters worse, gangs of outlaws roamed at large, and almost every day we saw shootouts, murders, and robbery.

We lived in near poverty, in a small house with one cow. We did have a horse, but when it died, we were left without an animal to pull the plow. In 1935, the situation became more unbearable—even our cow died—and my grandfather, who was over sixty, was forced to go from house to house, building stoves. Besides being a plowman, he was also a carpenter and cabinetmaker—a complete jack-of-all-trades.

In order to save the family, my father decided to leave the farm to find work on a construction site. It was then Stalin's so-called period of industrialization. He knew that construction workers would be needed for the building of a potash plant at Berezniki in the neighboring province of Perm, so he moved the family there. We all harnessed ourselves to the cart, loaded it with our few possessions, and set off for the railway station—itself a distance of twenty miles.

After we arrived at Berezniki and my father signed on at the construction site as a laborer, we were housed in one of the communal huts typical of that time—which, to this day, are still to be found in a few places—built of clapboard, through which drafts whistled relentlessly. The hut had a central corridor and twenty small rooms, naturally without any modern conveniences; there was only an outdoor toilet and water drawn from a well. We were given a few sticks of furniture, and we bought a goat to supply us with milk. My brother and my sister, the youngest, had already been born by then. The six of us, including the goat, slept on the floor, huddled together. From the age of six I was in charge of the household. This meant looking after the younger children— rocking my sister in her cradle and keeping an eye on my brother to see that he didn't misbehave. My other domestic

23

chores were boiling potatoes, washing the dishes, and fetch-
ing water from the well.

While my father labored on the building site, my mother,
a gentle and kind woman by nature, would help relatives and
neighbors by sewing clothes. Every night she would sit down
with her sewing—never taking money for her work. She was
grateful if someone gave her half a loaf of bread or some other
morsel of food.

My father was rough and quick-tempered, just like my
grandfather. No doubt they passed these characteristics on to
me. My parents constantly argued about me. My father's
chief instrument for teaching good behavior was the strap,
and he walloped me good and proper for any lapses. Whatever happened in our neighborhood—if a neighbor's apple
tree had been robbed or if someone played a nasty trick on
the German teacher in school—my father would not say a
word but would reach for the strap. My mother would weep
and beg him not to touch me. But he would firmly shut the
door and tell me to lie down. I would pull up my shirt and
lower my trousers. He would lay into me with great thorough-
ness. I always clenched my teeth and did not make a sound,
which infuriated him; then my mother would burst in, snatch
the strap away from him, pushing him aside and standing
between us. She always defended me.

My father was an inventor, and he was always working on
a new idea. One of his ambitions was to invent a machine
that would lay bricks. He would sketch it out, rethink it, make
calculations, and then produce another set of drawings; it was
a kind of will-o'-the-wisp that he was perpetually chasing.
Unfortunately, no one has yet invented such a machine, although even now whole research institutes rack their brains
over it. He would constantly describe to me what his machine
would be like and how it would work; how it would mix the
mortar, lay the bricks, clean off the surface mortar, and move

forward. He had worked it all out in his head and drawn the general plan, but he never managed to realize his idea.

We lived in that crowded wooden hut for ten years. Strange as it may seem, the people who lived under those conditions somehow managed to be good, friendly neighbors, especially when one considers that there was no sound insulation. If there was a party in the rooms—a birthday or a wedding—everyone could hear it. There was an old wind-up gramophone with only two or three records, and these were shared by the whole hut; I can still remember one song in particular: "Shchors the Red Commander marches on beneath the standard . . ." which the whole hut used to sing. Conversations, quarrels, rows, secrets, laughter—the whole hut could hear everything, and everyone knew everyone else's business.

Perhaps it is because I can remember to this day how hard our life was then that I so hate those communal huts. Winter was worst of all. There was nowhere to hide from the cold. Since we had no warm clothes, we would huddle up to the nanny goat to keep warm. We children survived on her milk. She was also our salvation throughout the war.

We all earned money on the side. Every summer my mother and I would go out to a nearby collective farm. We would be allotted several acres of meadowland, and we scythed the grass, stacked it, and prepared the hay, half of which went to the collective farm and the other half to us. We would then sell our half and buy bread at exorbitant prices.

That was how my childhood was spent. It was a fairly joyless time. There were never any sweets, delicacies, or anything of that sort; we had only one aim in life—to survive.

Despite these hardships, I always stood out from the other students—especially because of my energy and drive. From first grade on, I was elected class leader, even though I went to several different schools. I did well at my studies and got

top marks in my exams. But my behavior was less praise-
worthy. In all my years of school I was the ringleader, always
devising some mischief. In fifth grade, for instance, I persuaded the whole class to jump out the first-floor window,
and when our unpopular teacher came back, the classroom
was empty. She immediately went to the watchman at the
main entrance, who told her that no one had left the building. We had hidden in a small yard beside the school. When
we returned to the classroom we were given a zero for the
day. We protested. We said, "Punish us for our bad behavior,
but test us on the lesson—we know it." The headmaster arrived, organized a special class, and questioned us for about
two hours. We had learned everything by heart, and all of us,
even the weak pupils, answered every question correctly. In
the end, the zeroes were canceled, although we were given
the lowest possible mark for behavior.

Another of our adventures took place at the local stream,
the Zyryanka. In the spring, it would overflow its banks and
become a river, and logs were floated down it. I invented a
game to see who could run across floating logs to the far bank.
The timber tended to flow in a fairly tight mass, so that if you
judged it carefully there was a chance of being able to get
across—although to do so you needed to be extremely skillful. Step on a log and if it gave the slightest sign of rolling
over and you delayed for a second, you would be under water.
So you had to move really fast from one log to another, keeping your balance all the time and leaping briskly in order to
reach the far bank. The slightest miscalculation and it was
into the icy water, with nothing but logs above you, between
which you would have to try to push your head and gulp a
lungful of air, not sure if you would come out alive.

We also used to have fights, neighborhood against neighborhood, with between sixty and a hundred boys at a time
fighting with sticks, cudgels, or fists. I used to take part in
these fights, although I always got clobbered. When two solid

walls of opponents clashed head-on, however strong you
might be, you would always end up with several bumps on
your head. I achieved my broken nose, like a boxer's, when
someone whacked me with the shaft of a cart. I fell, everything went black, and I thought it was the end. But I came to
my senses and was carried home. There were no fatalities in
these fights, because although we fought enthusiastically, we
observed certain limits.

I was expelled from school once. It happened at my primary school graduation. About six hundred people were gathered in the assembly hall—parents, teachers, and pupils—in
an atmosphere of cheerfulness and elation. Everyone was
solemnly handed his or her diploma. Everything was going
according to plan, when I suddenly stood up and asked permission to speak. My exam results had been excellent, nothing but top marks in every subject, and for that reason I was
allowed up on the stage. Everyone thought that I would simply say a few gracious words. Naturally I had some kind words
to say to those teachers who had given us valuable instruction
that would help us in our lives and who had developed in us
the habits of reading and thinking. But then I declared that
our homeroom teacher had no right to teach children because she crippled them mentally and psychologically.

That awful woman might hit you with a heavy ruler, she
might stand you in the corner, she might humiliate a boy in
front of a girl. She even made us clean her house. Once, the
class had to collect food scraps from all over the district to
feed her pig. It was endless, and some of the children refused
to oblige her, but others submitted.

Briefly I described how she mocked her pupils, destroyed
their self-confidence, and did everything possible to humiliate
every one of us—I went for her tooth and nail. There was an
uproar. The whole event was ruined.

The next day the school board sent for my father to tell
him my diploma was being withdrawn and instead I was to be

27

given a so-called wolf's ticket: a little scrap of white paper that testified to my having completed the required seven years of primary schooling but stated below that I was deprived of the right to acquire a secondary education anywhere in the USSR. My father came home furious and reached for the strap—but at that moment, for the first time, I gripped him by the arm and said, "That's enough. From now on I'm going to educate myself." Never again was I made to stand in the corner all night, and no one ever took the strap to me again.

I refused to accept the decision of the school board and took my case up the education hierarchy: first to the district and then to the city education department. I learned for the first time what a local party committee was. I succeeded in getting a commission of inquiry set up, which investigated the work of that teacher and dismissed her from the school. She got exactly what she deserved, and I got my diploma back, although under the heading "Discipline," the word "unsatisfactory" glared out from the line of otherwise perfect grades.

I decided not to go back to that school and instead entered the eighth grade at Sverdlovsk's Pushkin School, of which I retain the fondest memories. The staff was excellent; and in Angonina Kohonina we had a superb homeroom teacher.

It was then that I began participating in sports. I was fascinated by volleyball and was prepared to play it endlessly. I liked the way the ball obeyed me, that I could return even the most difficult volley. At the same time I took up skiing, gymnastics, decathlon, boxing, and wrestling; I wanted to try my hand at them all, to do absolutely everything well. In the end, volleyball prevailed, and I started playing it seriously. I kept a ball with me all the time, even when I went to bed, when I'd sleep with my hand resting on it. As soon as I woke up I would start practicing by myself—spinning the ball on one finger or bouncing it off the wall and the floor. But because I was missing two fingers on my left hand, I had difficulty catching a ball, and I worked out my own unique method of catching.

This is the story of how I lost my two fingers: The Second World War had begun, and some of us who were too young to go to the front made our own pistols and rifles and even a cannon. We decided to steal some grenades in order to learn what was inside them. I volunteered to break into the local church, which was being used as an ammunition dump. That night I crept through three layers of barbed wire, and while the sentry was on the other side of the building, I filed through the mesh on a window and climbed inside. There I took two RGD-33 hand grenades with fuses and managed to make my way back unharmed (the sentry would have fired without warning). We went to a forest about forty miles away, and this time I volunteered to take the grenades apart. I told the other boys to take cover a hundred yards off; then I put the grenade on a stone, knelt down, and hit it with a hammer. I didn't realize I had to remove the fuse. There was an explosion—and two of my fingers were mangled. The other boys were unharmed. I kept losing consciousness while they took me to town. Gangrene set in. The hospital surgeons cut off the two fingers.

Every summer during my student days I worked to earn pocket money, and I also organized long class hikes. Each trip had a special objective: to find the source of a river, or to get to the mountains. The expeditions usually involved trekking several hundred miles with knapsacks and living in the forest for several weeks.

The summer after ninth grade, we decided to find the source of the river Yaiva. We spent a long time climbing up through the forest, knowing that the source was somewhere near the crest of the Urals. The food we had taken with us was soon gone, and we lived on what we could find in the forest, mushrooms and berries. The Urals forest is very fertile;

one can survive there for a considerable time. Far from any roads, we tramped for a long time through the virgin woodland. Occasionally we came across a little hut used by hunters, where we would spend the night, but more often we built our own brushwood shelter or simply slept in the open.

We did at last find the source of the river—a spring of natural hydrogen sulfide. Turning back, we descended a few miles to the first village, by which time we were pretty worn out. We knew we needed a boat to travel farther. We collected whatever each of us could offer—a knapsack, a shirt, a hat—more or less everything we had to trade for a boat. Then we went to a little cottage and gave our possessions to the owner, in exchange for a small wooden flat-bottomed boat. In this boat we floated downstream; we no longer had the strength to walk. As we were floating along, we suddenly saw a cave in the hillside above us. We decided to stop and explore it. The cave led us on and on, until it suddenly opened out and brought us to a point somewhere deep in the forest. We scouted around but could not figure out where we were. We were lost, and we had lost our boat too. We wandered around for almost a week. We had brought nothing with us from the boat, and since the region turned out to be swampy, with nothing but stunted saplings and undergrowth, it provided us with barely enough to eat, and no fresh water at all. We collected the murky swamp water and sodden moss in a shirt, squeezed it, and drank the liquid that dripped out of the shirt.

We finally managed to make our way back to the river, where we found our boat and were able to calculate our position, but the water we had drunk made us all very ill (eventually we were diagnosed as having typhoid fever). As the expedition leader, I stayed on my feet. I carried all the other boys down to the boat, laid them in the bottom, and, exerting my last ounce of strength to prevent myself from losing consciousness, steered the boat as it drifted downstream. I had only enough energy left to give the others some river water to splash over their faces, which were burning with fever. They lost consciousness, and soon I, too, began to pass out. When we reached a railway bridge that crossed the river, we thought that someone would find us. I moored our boat to the bank and collapsed unconscious. We were seen, picked up, and driven back to town; the school term had begun a month before, and search parties had been looking for us.

Typhoid fever kept us in the hospital for nearly three months. They had no medicines for it. My companions on the expedition had decided not to attend tenth grade—our last—that year and to stay on at school for an extra year. But halfway through the school year I began studying on my own at home. I worked day and night, and when the final exams began, I went to school to take them.

I arrived at school and was told I couldn't take the exams; there was no provision for home study in the final year. Once again, helped by the fact that this path was already familiar to me, I set off on a well-beaten track: all the local education departments and the party committee. By this time I was a member of the city's volleyball team; fortunately, I was also known as the junior champion in several sports and as volley-ball champion of Sverdlovsk province. In the end I was allowed to take the exams as an external student. Admittedly I did not get top marks in all subjects; I was given a four in two subjects, a five in all the others. That was my baggage for the onward journey to higher education.

As a boy, I had dreamed of attending an institute of ship-building. I had read a number of standard textbooks and tried to understand how ships were built. But gradually I began to be attracted by the profession of civil engineering—no doubt because I had already worked as a building laborer and because my father was in the construction business.

But before I could enter the department of civil engineering at Urals Polytechnic Institute, I had to pass one more test

—this one administered by my grandfather. He was over seventy by then, a most impressive man, with a long beard and a quirky, original cast of mind. He said to me, "I won't let you go into the building trade until you have built something with your own hands. You can build me a bathhouse. A small one, in the backyard, complete with a changing room."

We had never had our own bathhouse, though our neighbors did. Circumstances had always prevented us from building one.

My grandfather explained, "You must build it all yourself. My only contribution will be to get the local office of the State Timber Trust to allot you some trees in the forest. From then on you must fell the necessary pine trees, prepare moss for caulking the walls, clean it and dry it; you must carry all the logs from the forest yourself"—it was two miles—"to the place where you're going to build the bathhouse; you must make the foundations and do all the woodworking yourself, all the way up to the roof tree. And I," he said, "will not come anywhere near you." He was a stubborn old man, obstinate as they come, and he never once came within thirty yards of me. Nor did he lift a finger to help me, even though I found the work incredibly hard. When I had finished the bathhouse, my grandfather solemnly announced that I had passed the test and I now had his full permission to enter the department of civil engineering.

Although I hadn't done any special preparation for the entrance exams, because I had been building the bathhouse, I passed them comparatively easily, with two 80s, and 100s for all the other papers. During my first year I plunged into extra-curricular activities. I became president of the sports association, which meant I organized all sporting events. By then I was on the city's volleyball team, and after a year I was playing for Sverdlovsk in the senior league, which competed against the twelve best teams in the country. Throughout my five years at the polytechnic, I played, trained, and traveled all over the Soviet Union with the team. The strain, on top of my studies, was enormous. Unfortunately, we only reached sixth or seventh place in the league and never became the champions.

Altogether, volleyball took up about six hours of my day, and I could only study late in the evening or at night. I had schooled myself to do without much sleep, and I have managed to keep to that regimen ever since, sleeping for no more than three and a half hours a night. Volleyball has left a mark on my life, since I not only played but later trained four teams, including the men's and women's second teams of the Urals Polytechnic Institute.

After I finished the first year of studies at the institute, I decided to make a journey around the USSR. Until I entered the polytechnic, I had never seen anything of our country; I had never been to the sea and never traveled anywhere far from home. With no money in my pocket and little clothing —sweat pants, tennis shoes, shirt, and straw hat—I left Sverdlovsk. I carried a tiny suitcase of imitation leather, eight by twelve inches in size. It contained one clean shirt, and when I managed to buy food along the way by doing odd jobs, I would put that inside too. I began my trip with a fellow first-year student, but after a few days he realized that he wasn't up to our journey and he returned home. I went on alone.

I traveled by train, sometimes on the roofs of pasenger cars, sometimes on the open platform at either end of a car. Sometimes I hitched a ride on a truck. More than once I was stopped by the police, who would ask me where I thought I was going. I would say that I was going to see my grandmother in, for instance, Simferopol, in the Crimea. "On which street does she live?" Since I knew every Soviet town had a Lenin Street, I could never be wrong in giving that as my grandmother's address, and they would let me go.

I would travel by night, and when I arrived in a town—I naturally chose big, well-known places—I would spend the whole day, sometimes two days, exploring. I would sleep in a park or at a railway station before setting off again on the roof of a passenger car. From each town I wrote a letter to my friends at the polytechnic.

This was the itinerary I managed to complete: Sverdlovsk —Kazan—Moscow—Leningrad—Moscow again—Minsk—Kiev—Zaporozhye—Simferopol—Eupatoria—Yalta—Novorossisk—Sochi—Sukhumi—Batumi—Rostov-on-Don—Volgograd — Saratov — Kuibyshev — Zlatoust — Chelyabinsk — Sverdlovsk. I did that journey in a little over two months. I returned home in rags. My tennis shoes had lost their soles, and I was wearing them only for form's sake. I was actually barefoot, but it looked to everybody as if I were wearing tennis shoes. My straw hat, too, was worn to tatters, and I had to throw it away. You could see daylight through my sweat pants. When I had set out, I had also owned a big old-fashioned watch, a gift from my grandfather. But I had lost that watch, along with my clothes, in a game of cards at the very start of my trip.

It happened thus: An amnesty had been declared, and many newly released prisoners were returning home on the roofs of railway cars. One day several of them joined me up there and they said, "Let's play poker." This was a card game about which I knew absolutely nothing; I had never played cards in my life, and to this day I can't stand playing. But then I had no choice. They proposed playing for clothes, and very soon they had stripped me down to my underpants. They had won everything I had. Finally they said: "Now we'll play for your life. If you lose this time, we'll throw you off the roof of this car while the train's moving. We'll choose a spot where you'll land good and hard. But if you win, we'll give everything back to you." I still find it hard to understand what happened then, as I gradually began winning, first my hat, then my shirt, and finally my trousers. Either I had already grasped something about poker or they suddenly felt sorry for me. I ended up the winner. They gave everything back to me except my watch, and they never bothered me again; they even started to respect me. When they got hot water at the stations and made tea, they would share it with me. One of them even gave me a hunk of bread. They all left the train before we reached Moscow, and after that I was usually alone on the carriage roof.

In Zaporozhye, I remember, when I was nearly starving, I chanced upon an army colonel, who said to me, "I want to study at the local polytechnic, but I don't understand a damn thing about mathematics. Will you tutor me so I can pass the entrance exam?" He had been through the war and clearly managed to bring home a considerable amount of loot, because his flat was, for a mere colonel, richly furnished. I agreed but made it a condition that apart from three or four hours of sleep, we would work all the time. The colonel doubted that he could keep up with this pace, to which I replied that otherwise it would be impossible to prepare him for the entrance exam in the week we had before it was scheduled. My other condition was that he should feed me—and feed me well. His wife did not work outside the home, so she kept that end of the bargain. I ate my fill for the first time since leaving home, and I even put on weight. The colonel proved to be a dedicated student, a man of strong character, and he survived the pace of instruction I had set.

I heard later that he had passed his math exam and was accepted into Zaporozhye Polytechnic.

When I returned to school, my studies went well. With one exception, I got nothing but 100s in my exams, although volleyball continued to take up a lot of my time. And unlike students today, I was not allowed academic concessions because of my successes in sports. If anything, it was the reverse: Some of the lecturers were harder on me since they resented my enthusiasm for sports and believed that volleyball was distracting me from serious work.

One day, during an examination on the theory of plasticity, a professor proposed that I should answer one question straight off, without preparation. He said, "Comrade Yeltsin, take this piece of paper with the question written on it and try to answer it. You're a great athlete; why should you need any preparation?" Everyone had a notebook, because in the theory of plasticity there are certain formulas that take more than a page to write and are impossible to learn by heart, so we were allowed to refer to textbooks and notes. We argued over the issue for a long time, but he only gave me an 80, which was a pity. Yet generally he treated me well. One day I solved a very difficult problem that none of his students in the previous ten years had been able to master, and for that reason he developed a real affection for me. All the same, the one and only mark he gave me was 80.

My beloved volleyball all but brought me to the grave. At a certain point, both training for six to eight hours a day and studying at night (because in my final exams I wanted to get no grade less than "Excellent"), I overexerted myself. As a result, I fell ill with tonsillitis. I had a temperature of 104 degrees, but still I went on training. My heart couldn't stand it. My pulse was 150 when I collapsed and was taken to the hospital. I was told that if I stayed in bed, there was a chance that in a minimum of four months my heart would recover— otherwise I would develop heart disease. I discharged myself from the hospital after a few days. My friends made a rope out of sheets, and I lowered myself down it from the top floor of the hospital and took the train to my parents' home, in Berezniki. There I began slowly to recover, although whenever I got out of bed I would sway from side to side, and if I stood upright my heart would start pounding. But soon I began finding my way back to the gymnasium; all I could manage was a couple of minutes on the volleyball court before collapsing again. My teammates would carry me to a bench, and I would lie down. There appeared to be no way out of my situation; it seemed that my heart might be permanently damaged and my days as a player over. Nevertheless, I decided to fight. I began by going on the court for a minute at a time, then for two minutes, then five, and after a month I was able to last out a complete game. When I returned to Sverdlovsk, I went to see my doctor, and she said, "Well, even though you ran away from us, your condition is so good that you must have been in bed the whole time. Your heart is in excellent shape." I had taken a colossal risk, but it paid off.

As the time approached for submitting my graduation dissertation, I was away on tour; the national volleyball championships were in full swing, and our team was traveling from city to city. When I returned to the campus, there was only a month left in which to write my thesis. The topic was the construction of a television tower. In those days there were practically none built, so I had to research it from scratch. To this day I don't know how I managed to do it—everything myself, from beginning to end—all the drawings, all the calculations. Even so, my dissertation was accepted and marked "Excellent."

So my student years came to an end. Our class was a very close-knit group, and we made a pact that every five years we would spend our holidays together. Since 1955, when we graduated, thirty-four years have passed, and this tradition has not been broken. On one occasion, we even brought our children with us, and eighty-seven people came to that gathering. There was never any question of going to a resort or a hotel for our holiday. We have always roughed it: We have hiked across the taiga forest and through the Urals. Once we sailed down the Yenisey in Siberia as far as Dixon Island, in the Arctic Ocean, off the mouth of the Yenisey River. Each time we meet, we set up an organizing committee, which prepares our next gathering. For the first three occasions I was chairman of the committee, but when I became first secretary of the Sverdlovsk provincial party committee, my friends decided to release me, since I then had more than enough to do.

Over the years, relations among us have become amazingly close, warm, and heartfelt. Whenever I found myself in difficult situations, they have responded by offering me their support. One can safely say that these are real friends.

2

February 19, 1989

Chronicle of the Election Campaign

A start has been made. I have gotten past the nominating meeting. Now my election depends on the people. I was proposed as a candidate in nearly two hundred constituencies, and this support for me has come largely from big factories and other organizations that are thousands strong.

But such constituent support still counts for nothing. The nominating meetings, which are organized, conducted, and controlled by the apparat, allow it to eliminate any unsuitable candidates. A majority of these meetings, made up of so-called workers' representatives, were packed with party secretaries, their deputies, and members of workers groups, who have been "instructed" to the point of intimidation. Naturally it is no problem to manipulate such an audience, and from all corners of the country protests have come pouring in to the central electoral commission, declaring that the meetings usurped the people's right to hold real, meaningful elections. The authors of this charade, called the Election of People's Deputies, USSR, rubbed their hands together and delighted that their carefully laid plans had been put into effect so successfully.

Even so, they have miscalculated. Their plan has not been successful everywhere. They somehow failed to realize that even the secretary of a party committee might defect and vote as his conscience dictated; that even an obedient member of a workers collective might mark his ballot with the name of a candidate who was not the one he had been told to vote for.

The first nominating meeting I took part in was in the town of Berezniki in Perm province. I had once lived in that town, and people there still remembered me—and the name Yeltsin too, since my father worked there for a long time. Therefore my chances of passing the selection process were good—provided the party organization did not completely succeed in stifling the wishes of the meeting.

I decided to make an unusual move in order to surprise my opposition. After the last flight had left Moscow for Perm, I flew to Leningrad, where friends and supporters were waiting for me. They drove me out to a military airfield, where more of my followers waited. Next I flew to Perm, in a propeller-driven aircraft that roared and rattled so loudly that I was afraid I'd be deafened for life. I spent the journey embracing something that was either a cruise missile or a bomb. We landed at Perm early in the morning. There, too, I was met by trusted people, and I reached the nominating meeting just as it was to begin. My appearance was a shock to the organizers.

40

No local party members had yet arrived. I made a speech in which I presented my program and answered questions. Everything went splendidly, and when the voting began I had no worries about the outcome. It was evident from the atmosphere of the meeting that I would win the first round of the election. I got an overwhelming majority of the votes, then returned to Moscow to continue the campaign.

Next the nominating meetings began in the capital. Despite my success at Berezniki, I decided to participate in the Moscow meetings. I wanted to feel their atmosphere, to try to learn something about the mechanism by which the powers that be exert their influence on people. I found Moscow an excellent school.

I made a point of withdrawing my candidacy in constituencies where I would have competed with candidates whose honesty and competence I respected. In one district of Moscow, for instance, Andrei Sakharov was on the list of would-be candidates; I telephoned and told him I would withdraw my candidacy in his favor. As it turned out, my withdrawal was academic, since he was ultimately elected through being a member of the USSR Academy of Sciences, one of the "social organizations" entitled to nominate their own deputies to the Congress of People's Deputies; other such social organizations include the Communist Party and the trade unions.

Each constituency nominating meeting provided me with some new experience. When the mood of the audience was particularly hostile, I found it all the more challenging to bring them around. I could almost see the delegates overcoming their hypnotized fear of the local party leadership and the presidium, which was controlling it as a conductor controls an orchestra.

The nominating meeting of Moscow's Gargarin district was a revelation. Among the candidates were some very strong figures—the writer and commentator on social affairs Yuri Chernichenko, the military historian General Dmitri Volko-

gonov, the film director Eldar Ryaznov, the cosmonaut
Alexei Leonov, and others—ten in all. In their speeches,
each asked the assembly to confirm all ten candidates, so that
in the election the voters could decide for whom to vote.

Since each candidate's speech was powerful, emotional,
and convincing, the delegates began to become confused, to
split apart, so that they lost their will to choose the best candidates.

And then it began! The leadership tried one trick after another to prevent the delegates from accepting the proposal to
nominate all the candidates. The reaction was instantaneous.
Eldar Ryaznov was ready to explode with anger; some of the
electors ran up to the microphone and called shame on the
leaders, while others were chanting in chorus, demanding
that all the candidates be registered. This insulting treatment
of the selectors, the struggle between the people and the
brainwashed, programmed leaders, lasted until two o'clock in
the morning—when finally the people won. All candidates
were included in the electoral list for the constituency. I left
that meeting with a feeling of relief that fair play and common
sense had prevailed—but at the same time I was horrified.
What a terrible, pitiless machinery of power hangs over us all
—a monstrous instrument created by Stalin and Stalinism!

Tell us, is it true that after you graduated you went to work as a laborer on a building site? Why did you have to do that?

It's said that you were once put on trial in Sverdlovsk. Tell us what happened.*

An hour after the end of the oral examination for my dissertation, I was sitting on a train bound for Tbilisi to take part in the national volleyball championship. I traveled all that summer after graduation to play in matches—for the national championships, the interuniversity tournament, or the national league cup in Riga. I returned from the tour in September and started work at Uraltyazhtrubstroi (Urals Heavy Pipe Construction Trust), the organization to which I had been assigned after graduation.

* Questions from the floor at meetings during the election campaign.

43

I had been offered—as is every new graduate—a job as foreman on an industrial building site. I replied that I was not yet experienced enough to work as a foreman. While a student, I had come to the conclusion that although the teaching at the Urals Polytechnic Institute was of a high quality, some of the professors and lecturers were remote from the industry and taught their subjects in academic terms, which bore little relation to real life. I therefore considered it a great mistake to go straight into a job that put me in charge of men and construction work, without my having acquired direct experience. I was certain I would find life very difficult if any work-team leader could—deliberately or not—twist me around his little finger, since his practical knowledge of the job would be so much greater than mine.

I decided to spend a year learning the twelve basic trades. I would spend a month on each one. For a month I worked as an equal with others on a bricklaying team, where I learned all the techniques. And I worked one and a half or two shifts in a row, in order to gain experience more quickly. Even though the workers laughed at a young graduate's enthusiasm for getting his hands dirty, they helped me, encouraged me, and gave me moral support.

After I had spent a month at a trade, the appropriate official body would grade me according to my skill. Though usually I got a grade 3 or 4, I still acquired professional standing in each trade. Incidentally, I found the concrete-making particularly difficult: Although I am considered physically strong, pushing a wheelbarrowload of liquid concrete along narrow, high scaffolding is a very tricky job. If you allow the barrow to tilt, the center of gravity immediately shifts. There were times when I fell with the wheelbarrow, but fortunately it never ended in disaster, and in time I managed to acquire the necessary skill. I next learned the carpenter's trade, followed by a month of driving loads of concrete in a dump truck. Once there was a bad moment when I was driving a loaded truck, one that was far from new, with more than 180,000 miles on the odometer. It stalled right in the middle of a railroad crossing. The crossing had no gate and no guard. I could hear a train coming, and what's more, it was obviously coming fast. At any moment it would come pounding along and smash both the truck and me into smithereens. Then, luckily, I remembered the starter motor. When you engage the starter, the truck will jerk forward a little. By the time I had made a few feverish jabs at the starter, the train whistle was already hooting and its brakes were screeching, but I knew that it would not stop in time. The huge mass was heading straight for me, and I was still jabbing at the starter, making the truck lurch forward a little cach time. Finally it rolled a few inches off the track as the train passed by, missing me by a hair's breadth.

I climbed down from the truck, sat at the edge of the road, and struggled a long time to get my breath back. In spite of it all, I delivered the concrete safely and told the men how I had almost been killed. They said, "Well done! You did exactly the right thing." Of course, I could have jumped, but then I would have been held responsible for the loss of a valuable truck, and I had no savings. I had none then and I still have none, except for five rubles, which I deposited symbolically in a savings account during my student days.

While working as an operator on a crane, I had another nerve-racking experience. We were building an apartment house for Uralkhimmash (Urals Chemical Plant Trust). I thought I'd checked everything when I switched off the electric current one evening. But I had missed one check. When you close it down, the crane must be fastened to its rails with special hooks. But either I forgot or I had not yet been taught to do it—I don't know which. That night a pouring rain and a terrible wind woke me.

By this time I was married, and my wife and I lived right next to the construction site. Looking out the window, I saw to my horror that the crane was moving—slowly, but definitely moving. Just as I was—in nothing but my underpants —I bounded outside, ran to the crane, found the knife switch in the dark, and switched on the current. I climbed feverishly up the narrow steel ladder, as the crane rolled inexorably toward the end of the rails. I heaved myself into the operator's cab, which was pitch dark. Unable to see anything, after a moment's desperate thought I reckoned (correctly) that the first thing to do was to release the brake holding the jib. It immediately swung around into the wind and stopped acting like a sail. The crane's speed was slightly reduced, but it continued to move along the rails. Then I switched the crane's motor into full reverse. The crane began to slow down, and its wheels stopped a few inches from the end of the rails. It was an awful moment. I climbed down and fastened the essential hooks in position. But I could not sleep again that night, and for a long time I used to have nightmares in which I would climb up into a crane and crash to the ground with it.

After that came the other trades—carpenter, woodworker, glazier, plasterer, painter—none of which was easy to learn, but I was determined to pursue my original course.

At the end of the year I had learned the twelve specialized trades in the construction industry. I went to my boss and told him that I was now ready to work as a foreman. I helped build machine shops for the Uralkhimmash; a plant producing reinforced concrete; workshops for a factory at Verkh-Isetsk; subsidiary factory buildings; blocks of flats; a palace of culture; kindergartens; day schools and boarding schools—in other words, a lot.

Though I found the job as foreman relatively easy, I faced some new problems. For example, I had to combat pilfering, which had become very persistent. Building workers had got into this habit, until I started strict checks of every bricklaying job—measuring the amount of mortar, sand, and bricks

46

being used. Gradually I brought things under control, and my workers began to realize that I was right. The worker's conscience is not an empty phrase, so I was able to solve the problem.

There are times when we worked with convicts. I decided to break the tradition under which these men were paid at the rate they demanded instead of the normal rate. At the end of the first month, I calculated the volume of work they had done against the pay they should have gotten at the normal rates. It turned out to be two and a half times less than the amount they were used to getting.

Soon a hulking giant of a man came into my little foreman's office, carrying an ax, which he raised over my head, saying, "Are you going to pay us at the proper rate like they always paid us before you came along, you puppy?" "No," I said. "In that case," he replied, "you just remember that I've got nothing to lose. I'll smash your skull before you've even had time to squeak." I saw from the look in his eyes that he might easily have split my head open without batting an eyelid.

I could have dodged him or tried somehow to tackle him, but the room was cramped and the ax was already poised over my head. So I decided on an unexpected move. I have a very loud, powerful voice, and with great effect in that tiny room, I gave a sharp, full-throated roar of "Get out," while looking him straight in the eye. He suddenly lowered his ax, dropped it, turned around, and went out in silence, his back bent in submission. Exactly what went on in his mind at that moment is hard to say.

I was once sent as section chief to a unique site—a half-built worsted mill. It was a huge seven-story building, consisting only of a framework of reused steel girders that looked like a skeleton. It had been there a long time and was quite rusty, but instructions had come from above to develop light industry, and it had been decided to finish the building. I was put in charge of this complex project. I was living in a hostel belonging to the Chemical Plant Trust and had to walk from there to the site every day, a distance of eight or nine miles. I would leave at six in the morning and was usually on the job around eight.

Nearly a thousand men were working on the site, and when the city authorities added to the labor force, the numbers reached nearly two thousand. Work went on practically around the clock. That winter they were building a water tower: It was to be made by a unique method—entirely of concrete, including the water tank on the top. The concrete-pouring could not be stopped for a single hour: The concrete had to be heated during the mixing. For days on end I never left that water tower.

I worked on the site right up to the point at which we signed documents that transferred the mill to the worsted-spinning enterprise. When the whole job was handed over and the plant began operating, the building suddenly began to shudder and the whole massive metal frame, together with the reinforced-concrete cladding, started swaying in one direction. The looms had to be stopped. I went straight to my old teacher at the polytechnic. Together we surveyed and recalculated every element in the construction and came to the conclusion that there was a basic flaw in the design. The plinths supporting the sheathing were not strong enough to keep the building completely stable. We also found a second reason: The looms had been installed so that their movement was in one direction only. When they were switched on, the frequency of their vibration corresponded to the maximum vibration factor for the building, and it began to sway and shake. We solved that problem quite simply by repositioning the looms, which stopped the vibration, but the strengthening of the plinths took some time and gave us not a few headaches.

There was another critical situation, which I should mention. When the mill was within days of completion, it was

48

discovered that a fifty-yard passage from one building to another had not been built. Incredible, but true. The drawing for the passage had been mislaid! The factory was enormous, visible to the whole city, indeed to the whole country—it was due to produce six million yards of cloth annually. I immediately gathered together the best brains on the project, and we decided how the work on the passage should be organized. The whole discussion took only half an hour. Everything was calculated to the minute: so much time for the excavation work, so much time for the concrete-pouring and finishing, putting first one team and then another on the job. One excavator would start digging the trench, immediately followed by another. Each person was responsible for his or her own sector. I stayed on the site, never leaving it for a moment. By six o'clock the next morning, the asphalt was already being laid on that damned passageway. Soon the whole job was finished: We had made it!

Shortly thereafter, I was appointed chief engineer of construction directorate number 13. The general manager was Nikolai Sitnikov—an eccentric man, to put it mildly, obstinate and bad-tempered, whose obscenities at times went totally out of control.

We developed a strange relationship. He would arrive somewhere and start kicking up a fuss. If I thought I was in the right, I would refuse to give ground and would go on doing the job my own way. This would infuriate him. If I was in a car with him and having an argument, he would stop the vehicle in the middle of nowhere and open the door and say, "Get out!" "I won't get out. Take me to the nearest train stop." We would remain there for half an hour, even an hour, until he would give in because he was late for some appointment; then he would slam the door and drive me to a train. Other times, he would call me into his office and start to curse me up and down, saying this or that was wrong—then he would pick up a chair. I would do the same, and we would advance on each other. I would say, "Just remember that my reactions are quicker than yours, and if you make the first move I'll hit you first." Such was our relationship.

Several times he asked the City Committee of the Party to dismiss me, even though I had already reached senior status. But I had achieved a good working relationship with my colleagues, and the City Committee refused to get rid of me. In those days the second secretary was Fyodor Morshchakov, a likable and intelligent man, who came to my rescue on more than one occasion.

In the course of one year, Sitnikov reprimanded me no less than seventeen times—a new record. On December 31, I gathered up all these reprimands, went to his office, slammed them down on his desk, and said, "The first time you issue a reprimand in the new year I shall kick up an almighty row. I'm warning you." By January 2, I had already collected one for not working New Year's Day. January 1 is a public holiday, but according to my boss that didn't matter—I should have worked. I contested this reprimand and took my protest all the way up the official hierarchy. The reprimand was officially withdrawn. After that he was more careful.

Then he took me to court, having tried to catch me in an accounting error. The chief accountant, acting for the trust, was the plaintiff, and I consequently was the defendant. I sat in the witness box and proved that I had done nothing criminal or actionable. The judge was fortunately an intelligent man. In announcing his verdict to the court, he spoke as follows: "The actions of every manager may or must contain an element of risk. The chief aim is to ensure that such risk is justified. In the given case, the risk inherent in Yeltsin's actions was justified. The court has therefore decided that Yeltsin is fully acquitted and that the plaintiff is required to pay the cost of the case." Although the trust would bear the actual costs, this was a heavy blow both to the chief accountant and to Sitnikov.

The chief accountant did not forget his humiliation in court, and being a member of the party committee, he tried to trip me up during the interview I had to undergo as part of my application for party membership. He asked me on what page of which volume of *Das Kapital* Marx refers to commodity-money relationships. Assuming that he had never read Marx closely and had, of course, no idea of either the volume or the page number in question, and that he didn't even know what commodity-money relationships were, I immediately answered, half-jokingly, "Volume Two, page 387." What's more I said it quickly, without pausing for thought. To which he replied with a sage expression, "Well done. You know your Marx well." After it all, I was accepted as a party member. But the willful behavior of the general manager lasted until I was given the job of chief engineer at an industrial complex that was bigger than his trust.

Another severe reprimand I received was entered in my records in the office of the City Committee of the Party. I had become the head of a construction enterprise. The man who preceded me in the job was appallingly slovenly in his work and a drunkard as well. Any job that could be ruined, he ruined, including the one I was assigned to—the building of a boarding school, which was scheduled to be finished by the end of the year. In September, when I took over, they were still laying bricks for the first floor, and there were to be four floors. There was no hope of its being completed by the end of the year. At the beginning of the following year, I was received into the party by the district committee, and my membership card was issued at a solemn ceremony. The next day I attended the meeting of the City Committee of the Party, at which it published its report summing up the previous year. Suddenly I heard: "Let's give Yeltsin a severe reprimand to be entered in his records—just to teach the others a lesson."

I went up to the rostrum and spoke. "Comrade members

51

of the committee"—and there were a lot of them—"only yes-
terday you gave me my party membership card. Here it is,
still warm. And today you are proposing to give me—a Communist of one day's standing—a severe reprimand, to be entered in my records, for failing to hand over the boarding
school on time. There are other construction workers here,
and they will confirm that it was simply impossible to have
handed it over on time." No—the leaders insisted—it was to
be a lesson to others. Clearly, Sitnikov had had a hand in
this. It was a serious blow to me.

I believed sincerely in the ideals of justice that the party
espoused; with equal sincerity I had joined the party, having
carefully studied the party statutes, the program, and the
classics, reread Lenin, Marx, and Engels. And then suddenly
this had to happen at the City Committee. A year later, the
severe reprimand was annulled, but the entry would remain
in my records until the next regular review of party members'
behavior. It was only then that I had a clean sheet.

Only recently have we begun to recognize the negative
effects of the party's interference in economic affairs. In
those days, though, both people in the industry and, still
more, the party officials thought of this interference as a perfectly normal state of affairs. I thought so too, and regarded
it as quite natural when I was summoned to attend several
district committee meetings simultaneously. Of course, I
tried to wriggle out of these sessions, but the fact that they
took place at all—attempts were made to solve economic
problems by the application of political pressure and the issuing of reprimands—was part and parcel of the way the system functioned, and it never raised any questions or
objections. The main thing was to keep out of the way of
some nagging apparatchik, who, thanks to either stupidity or
megalomania, could easily make one's life a misery. I remember coming into contact with one Leonid Bobykin, first secretary of a district committee—the same man who was later

to become first secretary of the Sverdlovsk provincial committee and who at the Nineteenth Party Conference, in June 1988, was to hand up to the platform a note containing a ridiculous attack on a man who had spoken in my defense.

One day I got a telephone message from Bobykin ordering me to attend a meeting at a certain time. I was surprised at his tone—I don't know whether to call it lordly or boorish—and I did not reply to the message. Once, it was possible for me to be invited simultaneously to meetings of twenty-two separate organizations, beginning with the seven district committees and executive committees in those districts where we were engaged in building work, and ending with the provincial party committee. Naturally it was impossible to be everywhere at once: some meetings I would reschedule by telephone; to others I would send deputies. We juggled dates and times on a mutually acceptable basis. But now came a summons from Bobykin in this strange, hectoring tone. He sent me two more telephone messages. Finally he phoned me himself—would I kindly explain why I was not going to turn up at the meeting, which was being conducted by the first secretary of the district committee of the party? I asked him why I should go to his meeting in particular, if at the same time I had meetings in other districts; why should I give preference to him and not to someone else? This made him bristle with fury: "I'll report you! I'll damn well make sure you come." I replied, "After talking to me like that, you will never see me at one of your meetings again." And so it was that he couldn't do anything to me. He had only wanted to satisfy his self-importance . . . and he hasn't changed to this day.

After that job I was offered the post of chief engineer at a large, newly created house-building combine, which had its own factory and a work force of several thousand—which subsequently grew even bigger. When the general manager of the complex was retired on a pension, I was nominated to take his place. Thus, at the age of thirty-two, I found myself running a very large industrial complex.

It was a difficult time. I was simultaneously taking over the factory and introducing new technology, including a technique based on the flow principle to speed up the rate of construction. We also experimented with building a five-story apartment house in five days. Then, when we were constructing a new housing development composed of such buildings, we used tower cranes on one structure after another without dismantling the cranes: The tracks were extended from one building to the next. In this way we saved a lot of the time normally needed to dismantle and reassemble the cranes. There were other technical innovations, and the complex regularly began to meet its planning targets. We had special overalls embroidered "DSK" (the Russian initials for "House-Building Combine"), each made to order for the individual worker. Our people liked this very much, and they began to show pride in their firm.

My management style was generally regarded as tough. I required my people to maintain discipline and stick to their word once they gave it. Since I never swore and tried not to raise my loud voice, my main strengths in the battle for discipline were my own total dedication to the job, my insistence on high standards, and constant checking of work—plus people's faith in the rightness of what I was doing. I believe that people who work better live better and are more appreciated. Good, professional, high-quality work never goes unnoticed, just as spoiled materials, waste, and slovenliness don't go unnoticed either. If you've given your word, keep it—you must answer for it. These clear, understandable attitudes created, I think, a climate of mutual confidence between the management and the work force.

We had a carpenter named Mikhailishin, an excellent, skilled craftsman. On one occasion, I had to ask him to get us out of trouble. The government commission was coming to take over a building the next day, and although the doors had been painted, they needed to be turned around and re-hung. Through carelessness, the factory had put the hinges on the wrong side of the doors. We would deal with them later, but right then we had to save the situation. You couldn't go at the job like a bull at a gate. What was required was careful, neat, skilled work: The doors should not be marked, the floors should not be scratched. The job had to be done so that early the next morning, all that needed to be done was to repaint the hinges. I left him working on the job all night and came back at six o'clock the next morning. As I arrived, he was finishing off the front door at the main en-trance. I had brought my transistor radio with me, and I gave it to him; we embraced, and not another word needed to be said.

I also thought it was important to join one of the women's teams during the night shift and chat with them about this and that, help to hang wallpaper or paint window frames. This was a great boost for morale, both for myself and for them. What's more, it was of value for the project as a whole: I was able to identify apparently minor snags that, if the boss was not kept up-to-date about them, might blow up into huge unsolvable problems. Installing mirrors in the women's dress-ing rooms; purchasing dress material as a reward for good work; giving other gifts, bought either from trade union funds or, sometimes, out of my own pocket—all of this created a wholly different atmosphere in the relationship between man-agement and the women workers.

I had been working for fourteen years in the construction industry when I received an invitation to head the section of the provincial committee of the party responsible for con-struction. I was not surprised to receive this offer—I had been constantly engaged in party work outside working hours —and I accepted it. The work as head of a construction com-plex suited me: We were achieving our planned targets, and the work was going well. Plus I was getting a decent salary. Nowadays as a member of the Supreme Soviet I earn less than I did in that construction job twenty years ago. But I took on the party job just the same. I wanted to try to make a move in a new direction—though, to this day, I am still not quite sure exactly where that move led me.

3

February 21, 1989

Chronicle of the Election Campaign

It's strange, and I still can't believe it: I have been accepted as a candidate for Moscow deputy. What the apparat didn't want to happen and what they opposed so desperately has happened after all.

But to tell the story as it happened, I was supposed to have been blackballed at the nominating meeting. Of the one thousand people in the hall, only two hundred represented the ten candidates, while eight hundred had been carefully chosen—obedient, brainwashed selectors.

Everyone knew how the nominating meeting was supposed

to end: The apparat had nominated two candidates—Yuri Brakov, general manager of the automobile factory, and Georgi Grechko, a cosmonaut. My only real chance of nomination was that I might succeed in breaking the apparat's grip on the meeting and making sure that all three of us were chosen. Before the start of the meeting, the hopefuls, on my urging, signed a letter requesting that all of us be nominated as candidates. They signed the appeal very readily, since none of them wanted to participate in a charade whose outcome was rigged ahead of time. From the mood of the selectors, I sensed that this time the tactic wouldn't work. Only two names, Grechko and Brakov, had been hammered into the selectors' heads.

After each candidate had made a speech presenting his program, we were required to answer written questions for five minutes, followed by seven minutes of answering verbal questions from the floor. More than a hundred written questions were passed up to me.

I knew that the hall was filled with people who had been given provocative questions to ask me, and they were only waiting for the signal from the organizers to stir up controversy. I decided to use an unexpected method. Candidates usually choose to answer the most potentially favorable questions; I decided to do the reverse. Of the written questions put to me, I picked those that were most unfair, unpleasant, or insulting.

I began answering such questions as "Why did you let down the Moscow party organization with your cowardly failure to face up to difficulties?" and "Why was your daughter able to move into a new flat?" and so on, all in the same spirit, except that no one asked why I had been questioned by the police or whether I had any discreditable links with dubious figures. The answers that I gave ruined completely the plans of the people who had instigated these moves. Nearly all the hostile questions that they had expected from the floor had already been answered. I could sense the audience starting to thaw. It began to look as if the meeting might not end the way the organizers had planned it. We had arranged another surprise as well. Before the start of the proceedings, Georgi Grechko had approached me and said that he wanted to withdraw his candidacy because he thought I should be the candidate. I said, "All right, but think about it carefully." He replied, "I have definitely made up my mind." I asked him not to announce his withdrawal until immediately before the voting was due to begin.

Grechko played his part to perfection. Throughout the meeting he looked anxious and concerned, giving every appearance of being sincerely affected by the reaction of the selectors, the answers, the questions, and the procedural arguments. Then, just before the votes were to be cast, each candidate was given a minute to make a final statement. Grechko walked calmly to the rostrum and announced, "I wish to withdraw my candidacy."

This was, of course, a shattering blow to the organizers. All those who had been instructed to vote for Brakov and Grechko were suddenly faced with a real choice, especially since the vote was being taken by secret ballot. I collected more than half the votes, and the plans of my enemies failed.

I believe my enemies have often been frustrated because for some reason they think they are dealing with people who are bilious and ill-natured. They always base their tactics on an appeal to the rotten apples in the barrel, and there are too few of them. That is why they fail. If they had managed to fill the meeting with people like that, then there is no doubt I would have lost. But in all Moscow they could not find eight hundred people of their own ilk. What bad luck for them!

A new stage in the election campaign had now begun. I had cleared the first hurdle and my chances of winning had increased, but the resistance of those who saw my election as a catastrophe increased. I represented to them a collapse of faith in the unshakability of the established order. The fact that the established order had long since turned rotten did not worry them. The main thing for them was to keep Yeltsin out.

It seemed, though, that it was too late for that.

What mistakes did you make when you were first secretary
of a provincial committee of the party?

Was any criticism directed at you, and how did you react to
it when you were first secretary of the provincial committee
of the party?

The best years of your work as first secretary of a provincial
committee of the party were during the "era of stagnation"
[the Brezhnev years]. What are your feelings about this?*

I worked as a section chief in the Sverdlovsk provincial committee of the party, after which I was elected as a secretary of
the committee. Approximately a year later, I was sent to Moscow to attend a two-week course at the Academy of Social

* Questions from the floor at meetings during the election campaign.

61

Sciences. At the time, a full assembly of the Central Committee was being held, at which Ryabev, the first secretary of the Sverdlovsk provincial committee, was selected as a secretary of the Central Committee. The next day, during a lecture, the official in charge of our course came up to the microphone and announced that Yeltsin was invited to report in person to the Central Committee. The other students began to gather around me. We all wondered why I had been summoned. Though I wasn't certain, I did suspect what it might be. Trying not to be nervous, I left for the meeting at the appointed time.

I was told to go first to Kapitonov, the Central Committee secretary responsible for organizational matters. He asked me about my studies and my relations with colleagues on the committee. I told him that everything was going well. But he did not explain why I had been called. He said, "Now let's go and see Kirilenko." The meeting with Kirilenko was another empty conversation, ending in nothing specific having been discussed. Next I was taken to see Suslov. This time the tone was slightly less subtle and to the point: Did I feel up to a bigger job? Was I well acquainted with the party organization in the province? And so on. But there was still no mention of anything concrete. This is certainly a strange way of going about things, I thought. What does it all mean? Then I was told that Brezhnev wanted to see me. I was escorted to the Kremlin by two of the Central Committee secretaries, Kapitonov and Ryabev. We went into an anteroom, where an aide said to us, "Go in, you're expected." I entered first, followed by the others. Brezhnev was sitting at the far end of a big conference table. I approached him. He stood up, and we exchanged greetings. Then he turned to my "escort" and said, "So he's decided to assume power in Sverdlovsk province, has he?" Kapitonov explained that this was not so, as I still knew nothing of the proposal. "How can he not know, since he's decided to assume power?" So began our talk, half joking, half serious. Brezhnev said that the Politburo had been in session and had recommended me as first secretary of the Sverdlovsk provincial committee of the party.

At that time, Korovin was second secretary of the Sverdlovsk committee, but the usual procedure whereby the second secretary moves up when the job of first secretary becomes vacant was being disregarded. As a result, a rank-and-file secretary was being promoted to first secretary over the head of the second secretary, who would stay in place. Everyone realized that Korovin was unsuited for the job of first secretary.

"Well, what do you say?" Brezhnev asked. The whole matter was a surprise to me; the province is a very large one, with a correspondingly large party organization. I replied that if the Politburo and the provincial party members had confidence in me, I would do the job to the very best of my ability. We all stood up, and Brezhnev suddenly said, "For the time being, though, you will not be a member of the Central Committee; the Party Congress is over, and so elections to the Central Committee are also finished." Naturally I could not raise this point myself, but I felt encouraged by his tone of voice, which indicated his approval of me. Then he noticed that I wasn't wearing the red enamel lapel badge of a deputy of the Supreme Soviet and said, "Aren't you a deputy?" I replied, "Yes, I am." He looked around with astonishment at the two Central Committee secretaries: "What sort of deputy is he?" Quite seriously I said, "Of the provincial soviet." This, I must say, caused considerable amusement, because at the Kremlin level, a deputy of a provincial soviet is not considered to be a deputy at all. On that note we departed. "Don't take too long," said Brezhnev, "in getting him confirmed at the local party plenum."

Literally within a few days, on November 2, 1976, a plenum of the Sverdlovsk provincial committee of the party was held, at which Razumov, first deputy head of the organization department of the Central Committee, was present. Everything went as planned. Razumov announced that following Ryabev's election as a secretary of the Central Committee of the CPSU, Yeltsin was proposed as first secretary of the Sverdlovsk provincial committee of the party. I had meanwhile jotted down a few notes for a short speech, feeling that this would be required of me. The vote was, as usual, unanimous. After the congratulations, I gave my brief speech, outlining my program for the future. The main idea was simple: We should, above all, be concerned about *people* and their welfare, since if you treat people well they will respond with improved performance in whatever their occupation may be. This has remained one of my beliefs.

The fate of the second secretary needed to be resolved, because the new situation had made it psychologically very difficult for Korovin to continue in that position. He was offered the post of chairman of the regional trade union council, a job he was very glad to accept. All reassignments of personnel are a difficult, delicate matter, and each time I faced it I had to brace myself inwardly. A major renewal of personnel was needed throughout the province, especially in the key jobs. I proposed, for instance, that the chairman of the provincial executive committee (PEC), Borisov, should be retired on a pension.

The part played by the PEC under this man's chairmanship had been clearly unsatisfactory. He agreed with me and took his retirement. I needed a strong, intelligent person in that job. As I reviewed a list of people known to me, I remembered Anatoly Mekhrentsev, general manager of the ZIK-3 automobile factory, winner of the decoration Hero of Socialist Labor, with a master's degree and a state prize—he was already a man of considerable distinction. I also knew of his outstanding human qualities, his erudition, his rapid grasp of a situation, and his ability not to get bogged down in detail. In addition to all this, he was still comparatively young. I offered him the post. At first he refused it, then he promised to think it over. I put some pressure on him, and in the end he took the job. Gradually he gathered strength, and in time he became the best PEC chairman of all the provinces in our republic.

Thus I gradually built up my new staff, a strong and creative team. We drafted programs for all the main areas of responsibility, programs that were serious, far-reaching, and thoroughly worked out. Each program was aired at staff meetings of the provincial committee, then put into effect. Sometimes our meetings were closed. Then each member could put forward whatever demands he might have, including demands on me. I purposely set up this frank, businesslike modus operandi, so that critical remarks aimed at me could become a part of standard procedure. Even though I did not always agree with the criticisms, which were sometimes damaging to my self-esteem, I tried to train myself to take it.

This was a period of furious activity, and as always in my life, I drove myself harder than anyone else. Gradually others, too, began to work at this pace; some could keep up with it, including Mekhrentsev. Others could not maintain the pace and did less work, but I made no special demands on them. The chief thing was that they should do their utmost and produce results. Although there were constant arguments and discussions, they were always businesslike and constructive.

It became a tradition to meet, together with our wives, to celebrate public holidays. This kind of human contact had a good effect on our work. Our province contained forty-five towns (regional and rural centers) and sixty-three smaller townships, and I promised myself that I would visit every one of them at least once every two years. I kept that promise, and what's more, my visits were not just excursions but were taken up with serious work. I would meet local party activists, professional people, workers, collective farmers, and ordinary country folk. And I made sure that one of these traditional annual journeys always fell on my birthday.

I have always been embarrassed by effusive displays of congratulations on my birthday. And if I tried to hide at home or in the party office, I would have been discovered there anyway. So I would go to some distant region and meet people on farms, in the fields—anywhere I couldn't be found. I have never liked the traditional way of spending birthdays, when you sit at a table and people tell you to your face how wonderful you are. It makes me uncomfortable. But by getting far away from home, by helping people, by making this or that decision on the spot, I would have spent the day doing something useful, and thus have given myself a birthday present.

I was always trying to think up ways to make our people proud of our province, so I was disturbed when, in his book *Tomorrow—Into Battle Again*, written after his victory over Viktor Korchnoi, the chess champion Anatoly Karpov directed a gentle but justified reproach at Sverdlovsk province. He regretted that a region as large as ours had no chess club. I telephoned Karpov and suggested that we agree on a date when he might visit us—and said that by then there would be a Sverdlovsk chess club. We made the arrangement, and work began. An old house was vacated and completely renovated; adjoining rooms were added; the result was a decent enough chess club. I sent a telegram to Karpov, saying that I was expecting him. He arrived with the cosmonaut Sevastianov, who was also president of the national chess federation. At a large gathering of people, I asked Anatoly Karpov to cut the ribbon, since he was the man behind the project. Beforehand I had told our local chess players that they should letter on a large sheet of drawing paper the quotation from Karpov's book about there being no chess club in Sverdlovsk. After he had made his speech, I handed him this banner and suggested that he tear it into little pieces—and, further, that he promise to make a correction in the next edition of his book so this shameful stain would no longer degrade our province. To the delight of all present, Karpov tore the sheet into tiny bits. And that was how a chess club was established in Sverdlovsk.

I kept up my personal sporting activities following my appointment, not as a member of a particular team but instead on a volleyball team organized from staff members of the committee. Soon it became hard to imagine life in the Sverdlovsk provincial committee without volleyball. We played twice a week, Wednesdays and Sundays, at half past seven till ten or eleven at night. Whole families took part; the contests were highly emotional. In fact, I would say that there was more excitement and enthusiasm than actual playing. Even so, I did stop participating in other forms of sport—except, of course, my daily exercises.

From the very beginning of my work as first secretary, I would organize meetings of various kinds of workers: school headmasters and teachers, for example; one thousand workers in the health service; fifteen hundred students; fifty leaders of the Young Pioneers youth organization; industrial foremen; factory managers; district party secretaries; young party workers—or those with long service and a lot of experience; the chairmen of district soviet executive committees; writers and artists; social scientists; academics—as many groups as I could find. In the Brezhnev "era of stagnation," such meetings were uncommon, because no one liked to answer difficult questions. If meetings were held at all, they were in honor of a great leader, a marshal of the Soviet Union, a much-decorated hero, et cetera.

Brezhnev did not concern himself with the country at all—or rather, he concerned himself with it less and less. The secretaries of the Central Committee followed his example, so we found ourselves working completely on our own. We did receive occasional instructions, but they were pure eyewash, issued merely for the record. Whenever we went to

Moscow to get a decision on a matter that we did not have the authority to decide for ourselves—a major construction project, for instance, or matters concerning food supplies or funds—we would naturally go straight to the man in the Central Committee responsible for our province: in our case, a sector chief named Pavel Simonov. Simonov was, incidentally, the perfect man for the job; while adopting an attitude of noninterference in our party organization, he was at the same time thoroughly well informed about our affairs, always knew what was happening and what our problems were. He would phone us now and again, sometimes to tick us off in a jocular tone, and altogether we enjoyed an excellent working relationship.

At the very start of my term as first secretary, Simonov gave me a memorable lesson. There was an exhibition of propaganda posters in town; I went to the opening, and our group was photographed as we entered the hall. This photograph was published in our local party newspaper, the *Urals Worker*. The next day I got a phone call from Simonov, and he began to teach me my lesson. He certainly knew how to do it; never raising his voice, he was thoroughly sarcastic at my expense. "Oh," he said, "how good you look in that photograph— really very good indeed. You're so photogenic, aren't you, and now the whole province will know how good you look in a photograph." He went on and on in that vein. He could really get under one's skin without ever being actually rude or nasty. I have remembered his lesson ever since. My picture never again appeared in a local newspaper.

But people like him are the exception in the Central Committee. When Ryzhkov was appointed chairman of the Council of Ministers, I tried not to abuse our long-standing acquaintance.

Here's a typical example of how the country was run in those days. We needed to get a top-level decision on the construction of a subway system. Sverdlovsk was, after all, a city of 1,200,000 inhabitants. We needed permission from the Politburo, and I decided to go to Brezhnev. I phoned him, and he agreed to see me. I had been told how to handle him, so I prepared a text to which he had only to add his signature in approval. I went into his office and we talked for literally five or six minutes. (It was a Thursday, usually the last day of Brezhnev's working week; as a rule, he would be driven on Friday to his enormous dacha at Zavidovo, where he would spend Friday, Saturday, and Sunday. So on Thursdays he was in a hurry to finish up his work. He was incapable of drafting the document himself. He said to me, "Just dictate what I should write." So of course I dictated it to him: "Instruction by the Politburo to prepare a draft decree authorizing the construction of a metro in Sverdlovsk." He wrote what I had said, signed it, and gave me the piece of paper. Knowing that even with Brezhnev's signature, some documents might be misplaced or disappear altogether, I told him, "No, you should call your aide." He summoned an assistant, and I said to Brezhnev, "Give him instructions that he must first enter the document in the registry and then take the necessary official steps to ensure that your instructions to distribute it to the Politburo members are carried out." He did all this; the aide collected the papers; and Brezhnev and I said goodbye.

The incident was typical and revealing. In the last phase of his life, Brezhnev, in my opinion, had no idea what he was doing, signing, or saying. All the power was in the hands of his entourage. He had signed the document authorizing the construction of the Sverdlovsk metro without giving any thought to the meaning of what I was dictating. Granted, as a result of that signature a good deed was done and Sverdlovsk soon received permission to build a metro. But how many of the rogues and cheats, indeed plain criminals, who surrounded Brezhnev exploited him for their own dishonest purposes? How many resolutions or decrees did he calmly, unthinkingly sign, bringing riches to a few and suffering to many?

But we are now well aware of the scale of favoritism and corruption in the Brezhnev era and the extent to which this caused the whole government to rot from within. The word of a first secretary is law, and no one would dare not carry out his order or request, so much so that unscrupulous party officials and their henchmen abused their power unchecked. Knowing my character, nobody ever approached me as first secretary to ask favors. It is hard to imagine how I would have reacted to any such request.

Yes, the power of a first secretary within his province is practically unlimited. And the sense of power is intoxicating. But when you try to use it for the public good, even that power is insufficient; it cannot, for instance, ensure that everyone in the province is decently fed and housed. It can fix up someone with a good job, make sure that someone else is allotted a nice flat, and hand out similar favors to one's immediate colleagues. So it has been in the past, and so, indeed, it continues to be. A few dozen people live in the ideal conditions that are predicted as universal when we have reached the stage of "full communism," while the population as a whole lives in conditions that are barely tolerable.

In those days a provincial first secretary of the party was a god, a czar—master of his province—and on virtually any issue the first secretary's opinion was final. I used that power, but only in the name of the people, never for myself. I made the wheels of the economic machinery turn faster. I was listened to and obeyed, and thanks to that, it seemed to me, every enterprise functioned better.

One area I never interfered in was the law, the courts and the prosecutor, except for one occasion when I had to intervene on behalf of a manager of a ball-bearing factory who had been indicted for not controlling the inventory at his factory. I empathized with him, especially as I had held managerial jobs in industry myself and knew all about the endless regulations. He was a good man trying to do his best, and it would have been a shame to lose him. There was nothing corrupt in what he had done; in part he had been let down by others, and in part he himself was to blame. But even so, he had not broken the law. After a careful examination of his case, he was found innocent.

When the next party congress was due to be held, I carefully prepared myself to attend it, for I wanted to address the appalling stagnation the country found itself in. I delivered a fiery speech, which stood out in contrast to the general chorus of adulation for Brezhnev but did not have the effect I had hoped for. I lacked not only sufficient experience but, more important, enough political courage to take a decisive stand against our rotten system of rule by the party bureaucracy. In addition, I did not yet know any members of the Central Committee well enough to be able to exert a significant influence on affairs, although I could already see that those in power were simply failing in their jobs.

Gorbachev and I first met when we were both working as first secretaries, he at Stavropol and I at Sverdlovsk. Our first conversation was on the telephone. Quite often we needed to extend each other a helping hand, exchanging metal and timber from the Urals for food products from Stavropol. He seldom gave us anything over and above the limits imposed by Gosplan, but he did help us build up our stocks of poultry and meat.

When in 1978 he was elected secretary of the Central Committee for Agriculture, I greeted his appointment with enthusiasm. I visited him from time to time because farming was difficult in Sverdlovsk province, owing to our unreliable climate and rocky soil. I devoted perhaps half my working hours to agriculture, never certain of reaching a consistent output, even though during my ten years in office there was certainly an increase in agricultural production.

Whenever I entered Gorbachev's office, we would embrace warmly; our relationship was a good one. I think that when he first came to work at the Central Committee, he was different than he is today—more open and frank. He very much wanted to improve agricultural matters; he worked hard at it and kept in contact with the outlying republics and provinces. We thought that at last Soviet agriculture might really get moving, but it did not happen. Gorbachev failed to grasp the essentials of the problem, and his hasty attempts to improve matters did not produce any decisive changes for the better.

When Gorbachev was secretary for agriculture, an incident occurred that may well have marked the beginning of a certain cooling in our relationship. A commission of inspection (there were a lot of them at the time) came to Sverdlovsk from the Central Committee to check on the state of affairs in the province. Understandably, in addition to our successes, the commission found problems that certainly existed, but their final report contained some obvious errors. The secretariat of the Central Committee issued a brief resolution based on the report and, what's more, issued it without first asking for my comments. We were simply sent the resolution, which was followed shortly after by a visit from Gorbachev's deputy, Kapustyan. Our party leaders were assembled, and Kapustyan made a speech echoing the tone of the resolution. Then I spoke. While agreeing in general with the conclusions drawn by the commission, I said there were certain points in the resolution that I could not accept, and I listed them. It was unheard-of to challenge a document of this nature, and there was an awkward silence. Then Kapustyan spoke again, and I replied even more sharply. The upshot was that before long I was summoned to Moscow.

That commission caused me a lot of worry. I tossed and turned at night, wondering whether I was right or wrong to stick to my own point of view. Kapustyan and Razumov, deputy director of the personnel department of the Central Committee, had prepared a memorandum officially notifying the members of the Central Committee that Comrade Yeltsin had not made a sufficiently objective appraisal of the problems in his province, had contested certain conclusions drawn by the commission, and had objected to various points made in the secretariat's resolution, thereby violating party discipline.

I learned about the existence of this memorandum before I reached Moscow, so I was not surprised to find Kapitonov waiting to see me when I arrived at the Central Committee. He began in a somewhat apologetic tone: "Boris Nikolayevich, there is a memorandum to the Central Committee from two departments that I've been asked to, well, not exactly discuss with you but make sure you know the contents of." He handed me the memo. I read it and immediately repeated what I had said at the meeting of the provincial committee—that I disagreed with several of the conclusions drawn by its authors. Kapitonov did not raise any other matters, and so we parted.

On the same visit I also went to see Gorbachev. He greeted me as though nothing had happened. We talked, and only as I was leaving did he say, with a hint of disapproval at what I had done, "Have you read that memorandum?" "Yes, I have," I said. Gorbachev replied, curtly and firmly, "You should draw the necessary conclusions!" I said, "Conclusions must indeed be drawn from the resolution, and I am doing that, but I am not obliged to draw any conclusions from the subjective, inaccurate statements made in the memorandum." "No," said Gorbachev. "You're wrong. You should take note of that memo all the same." But the matter ended there.

On that occasion, as always, Gorbachev addressed me in the familiar *ty* form of "you." But I have yet to meet anyone whom he addresses as *vy*, the polite, more formal form of "you" in Russian, equivalent to the French *vous*. He uses the familiar *ty* with all the older, senior Politburo members, like Andrei Gromyko, Vladimir Shcherbitsky, and Bitaly Borotnikov. Whether this is a lack of culture or a mere habit is hard to say, but whenever he addresses me as *ty* I feel a sense of unease. Inwardly I object to this form of address, though I never mentioned it to him.

On many occasions in the past when my frankness might have got me in trouble, I was saved by the fact that my speeches did not reach the ears of the top leadership. Simonov, the Central Committee watchdog over our province, would gather everything up and quietly consign it to the archives.

I also got on well with the members of the military council of the Urals military district. I frequently visited army and air force units, where I met both officers and men and attended training exercises. I was usually accompanied by members of the party, who would sometimes drive tanks and learn about aircraft. We helped the military get their camps and barracks rebuilt; this was necessary because conditions were terrible in some of the camps. The Ministry of Defense seems to regard soldiers as its slaves, who are supposed to keep their mouths shut. At a meeting held at one division, I asked for the first time why the soldiers never spoke up about the conditions under which they lived. Had they nothing to say? Their reaction was puzzlement, but naturally my comments filtered up to the officers. I continued to pursue this line, and gradually, through the Young Communist Movement (Komsomol) and the party network (rather than through strictly military channels), changes began to take place. The Komsomol members pulled themselves together, and eventually, at party meetings and other encounters with the military, critical remarks aimed at senior officers began to be heard. I regarded this change as essential.

I also developed reasonably good relations with the provincial directorate of the KGB. The head of the directorate, General Kornilov, used to take part in sessions of the party bureau as a candidate member. I frequently visited his department, asked for information about the work of the KGB, studied the way it functioned, and acquainted myself with every one of its branches. I knew, of course, that there were certain matters he kept secret from me. Even so, I got to know the KGB's system pretty thoroughly. Precisely for that reason, my speech at the summer 1989 session of the Supreme Soviet, when Kryuchkov was confirmed as head of the KGB, was not an accident. I did, after all, know a lot about the KGB, which is normally kept from all outsiders.

This knowledge was helpful when a tragic outbreak of anthrax occurred in our region during my early years as first secretary. The deputy chairman of the KGB, V. V. Pirozhkov, came to Sverdlovsk to investigate. Three of us—Pirozhkov, Kornilov, and myself—were seated in my office discussing the situation, and Kornilov remarked in passing that the local KGB directorate was collaborating closely with the provincial committee of the party. Suddenly Pirozhkov barked out, "General Kornilov, stand at attention!" Kornilov leapt to his feet and stood rigidly at attention. I was puzzled by this drama. Then, rapping out each phrase, Pirozhkov said to Kornilov, "Now get this into your head, General! In no part of your work, whatever it may be, are you supposed to 'collaborate closely' with the party organization. You are obliged to operate under its direction, and in no other way." A most instructive scene, I thought.

Kornilov became very depressed about this implication that he and his men were not doing their jobs properly. "In a region like this, you might think there'd be at least one spy, but there's not one," he would complain wistfully.

One of our worst emergencies was the accident at Bieloy-arsk nuclear power station, which took place during the night of December 31, 1978, and the morning of January 1, 1979, when the temperature was minus 57 degrees centigrade. A few metal structures in the generator building collapsed, and as they fell they struck a spark, igniting some oil.

Firefighting crews from Sverdlovsk displayed tremendous courage and heroism. They had to work in gas masks, because burning plastic gave off such thick acrid smoke that breathing was impossible. Most important, the fire had to be kept from reaching the reactor building. Hundreds of buses were held on standby to evacuate the nearby village, but the firemen, together with other specialists, succeeded in putting out the fire and saving the power station.

Many lives were saved as well. During the war, 437 factories had been moved to our area from German-occupied territories, and their workers were housed in dugouts and huts, some of which remained. Our region contained more people living in wooden huts than almost any other part of the country.

I have already described my feelings about these wooden huts. Since I dwelt in them nearly ten years of my life, my memories of those appalling shacks, inhabited by anywhere from ten to twenty families, depress me even today. People should not have to live in such conditions in the twentieth century, yet when I was put in charge of Sverdlovsk province, many families were still accommodated in huts. Soon afterward, a Politburo resolution was passed ordering the huts demolished throughout the country within ten years. It was obvious to me that people would not tolerate such a long wait; we had to put an end to the matter much sooner, once and for all.

I asked for the calculations to be done. It turned out that we would have to build about two million square meters of living space in order to move all the people living in huts.

Two million was an impossible figure. The entire province built only two million square meters of housing a year, and the waiting list included the disabled, large families, and war veterans, as well as many lower-priority categories.

I had to make a difficult decision. The choice was between the not very good and the downright bad. Which was more important—to get people out of the huts and freeze the waiting list for a year, or to continue to subject people to the torments of living in inhuman conditions, while housing all the others on the waiting list?

We decided to freeze the waiting list, which meant that for a year, only those living in huts would be moved. The others had to understand that the time had come to help those who lived in the worst conditions of all. And indeed, people did understand this—although I had to explain the situation to them and explain some more. Even so, many factory managers sent up howls of protest. Our new policy was a serious blow to them, for they were responsible for housing their workers. Arguments based on moral considerations left them cold. But I comprehended their attitude; as a former industrial manager, I knew very well just how important decent housing was for the morale of a work force, how eagerly it was awaited. And now the accommodations originally earmarked for their workers had to be given to someone else. It was a hard pill to swallow.

In order to save the situation, I made a trip to Moscow. I saw Kirilenko and explained the matter to him, saying that if he received complaints and curses directed at me because of our housing policy, he should put the complaints on file and be patient for a year. We simply had to get rid of those wooden huts. He agreed. Then I went to see Kosygin.

I described the situation to him and explained that I wasn't asking any favors: We required neither extra building materials nor additional industrial capacity—all we needed was moral support. Kosygin accepted my arguments; we agreed to

77

present the case jointly to a session of the full Council of Ministers and to ask the ministers responsible for each branch of industry to disregard any complaints coming from managers in Sverdlovsk province.

And it happened as we had foreseen. While we demolished one hut after another, the managers protested and wrote letters attacking me. Within a year all the former hut dwellers had moved into new, decently furnished apartments. And later, the provincial executive committee compensated most of the enterprises that had lost their housing allocation for that year.

If I had to choose the most remarkable achievement during my ten years as first secretary, I think it would be the building of the Sverdlovsk-Serov highway. The territory of the province is roughly the shape of an upturned heart; from north to south the distance is 312 miles. There was no highway between the cluster of large industrial towns in the north and Sverdlovsk and Nizhni Tagil in the center. The northern region is rich: There is bauxite, iron ore, and precious metals; there are metal working industries; there are the coal mines at Karpinsk and Tura. To travel by rail from Karpinsk, Serov, Severo-Uralsk, and Krasnoturinsk to Sverdlovsk used to take ten days. People were effectively cut off from normal life. The idea of linking these northern towns with the center by a highway had long been considered, but the task itself was extremely difficult. The highway would have to cross swamps, ravines, mountains, and several rivers. The distance is 220 miles. Owing to the difficult terrain, the cost per mile was astronomical. So we had to find enormous amounts of money for materials, wages, and equipment. We had no idea where to start. Meanwhile the need for the highway was growing more acute every year.

We asked the central planning authorities to allocate the funds to us. Their refusal came back very quickly. We called a meeting of all district and city first secretaries, chairmen of city and district executive committees, and other leaders in the province, in an attempt to find a solution. Could we raise the funds by pooling all our resources? We finally decided that we would build the road ourselves. We agreed to divide it into sections, allotting the responsibility for each section to particular towns; the towns would then form teams of road builders, and each team would build its own segment of highway.

This cumbersome operation could be made effective only if there was a clearly defined system for organizing the labor force as well as strict discipline and constant supervision. We set up a special headquarters to keep permanent watch on the progress of the work. We would drive up to the sections of highway or fly by helicopter to places that could not be reached by other means. Building the road was tough going, through swamps and peat bogs and over cliffs. I felt that nature was doing everything it could to stop us. Even so, the road was built to high standards, with a surface that was designed to last for many years.

When we were about a year away from completion, we named the month, the day, and even the hour at which the route would be opened. On that day, we would fill a fleet of hired buses with the leading party and soviet officials of the regions through which the highway passed, and set off along it in convoy. Anyone whose allotted section of road was not ready in time would have to get out. And some had to do just that. I am happy to report that since then this creation of all the people of Sverdlovsk province, the Sverdlovsk-Serov highway, has indeed appeared on the map. It was our joint, shared victory, and therefore especially dear to us.

I have never had any particular wish to enumerate the successes and achievements of my time as first secretary. I didn't do so even after Ligachev's attack on me at the Nineteenth Party Conference, in which he insisted, "Boris, you are wrong," and declared that I had made a mess of my job at

Sverdlovsk. Everyone, in my view, realized that this was a lie, and I considered it simply beneath my dignity to argue with him and prove the contrary.

Yet I did gain satisfaction from the fact that the food supply was improved, that we demolished the wooden huts, and that we built the Sverdlovsk-Serov highway. But there is one aspect of that triumph that still troubles me. To make senior city officials get out of the bus for all to see is not very kind. Indeed, it is typical of the notorious command system of running the economy by administrative fiat. In this particular instance it worked.

Nowadays, in the era of *glasnost*, there has been much talk about the Ipatiev house in Sverdlovsk (in czarist days known as Ekaterinburg), in the cellar of which the ex-czar Nicholas II and his family were executed by a firing squad in 1918. It was while I was first secretary that the Ipatiev house was destroyed, and this is how it happened.

People have always come to look at the Ipatiev house, although it was not very different from the other old houses in the neighborhood. The tragedy that occurred there in 1918 drew people to the place; they would peer through the windows or simply stand and stare in silence at the old house.

The Romanov family was executed as a result of the decision by the Urals regional committee of the party, and it was to the provincial archives that I went to read the relevant documents. Until quite recently, the facts of this crime were hardly known to anyone. But I believe the country wants to know the truth about its past, including the terrible truths. I was familiar with a falsified version, written in the spirit of Stalin's Short Course in the History of the Bolshevik Party, so it can easily be imagined how eagerly I read through the 1918 documents. Recently some documentary accounts of the last days of the Romanovs have been published in the Soviet press, but at the time I examined the archives, I was one of the very few people to have access to the secrets surrounding the execution of the czar and his family. It made painful reading.

At around this time, the results of the new research into the life of the last czar were published in Western newspapers and magazines. Some of this material was broadcast in Russian by Western radio stations. The new information stimulated interest in the Ipatiev house, and people even came to look at it from other cities. I reacted quite calmly, since it was obvious that the interest was caused neither by monarchist sentiments nor by any urge to install a new czar. The motives were curiosity, compassion, and a tribute to memory, which are normal human emotions.

Information about the large number of pilgrims visiting the Ipatiev house, however, found its way to Moscow. I don't know what machinery this information set in motion, what our ideologues were afraid of, or even what conferences and meetings were held, but I soon received a letter from Moscow marked "Secret." Reading it, I couldn't believe my eyes. It was a decree of the Politburo, adopted in closed session, ordering the demolition of the Ipatiev house in Sverdlovsk. Since the order was secret, the provincial committee of the party would be blamed for this senseless decision. Let me ask here when the Central Committee will decide to publish all the decrees of the Politburo, both secret and open. In my view, that time has already come. Much would then be revealed, and much that has been hitherto inexplicable would be explained.

But to continue, at the very first discussion of the matter in the provincial party bureau, I met sharp opposition from my colleagues to this order from Moscow. But it was impossible to disobey a secret decree from the Politburo, and in a few days' time the bulldozers were driven up to the Ipatiev house in the middle of the night. By the next morning, nothing was left of the building. The site was covered with asphalt.

What we had witnessed was yet another sad episode of the

81

Brezhnev "era of stagnation." I can well imagine that sooner or later we will be ashamed of this piece of barbarism. Ashamed we may be, but we can never rectify it.

I was brought up in the system; everything was steeped in the methods of the command system, and I, too, acted accordingly. Whether I was chairing a meeting, running my office, or delivering a report to a major meeting—everything one did was expressed in terms of pressure, threats, and coercion. At the time, these methods did produce some results, especially if the boss in question was sufficiently strong-willed. Gradually, though, I became more and more aware that what had seemed to be reliable and correct instructions issued by the party turned out, on checking, not to have been carried out at all; that more and more often when party officials or industrial managers gave their word that a thing would be done, it was not done. The system was clearly beginning to fail.

Toward the end of my decade in office, it seemed we had stretched ourselves to the utmost, that we had tried every possible method, every conceivable way of getting things done. It became more difficult to find new approaches, even though we continued to hold a special gathering of the staff at the beginning of each year in order to explore new working methods to be introduced into the party and, indeed, into every other organization in the province. Yet I nevertheless felt—although I never admitted it to anyone—that my satisfaction in the job was beginning to diminish. Our stock of ideas and methods had been exhausted. Whatever the cause may have been, I caught myself giving way to a feeling of wariness, of being up a blind alley.

My parents, Klavdia Vasilievna and Nikolai Ignatievich, and I, in a photo that belies our difficult times.

Here I am with my younger brother and parents.

My sister was the baby of the family, and I was in charge of her.

Students relaxing.

Provincials in Moscow.

My duties as coach of the women's volleyball team at the polytechnic institute kept me very busy.

Carrying my firstborn, Lena, at the 1960 May Day celebrations.

Even as first secretary in my province, I pitched in at potato harvest time.

С САХАРОВЬ

I campaigned passionately for Andrei Sakharov in 1989.

Sports have always been very important to me, and I miss them when I'm unable to play.

My wife, Naya, my daughter Tanya, and my grandson, Boris. I was honored that he was named after me.

Making a point while Lenin
looks on.

Some fans go to extreme
lengths; an icon in my honor.

I thank Yuri Kazannik for
ceding his seat on the Supreme
Soviet to me.

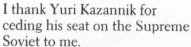

A rare moment alone with daughter Tanya.

Cross-country skiing with friends in Sverdlovsk.

4

February 22, 1989

Chronicle of the Election Campaign

The preelection nominating meeting in Moscow came to an end at about three o'clock in the morning. Three hours later, I flew back home to Sverdlovsk. I had given instructions to my close friends to send telegrams to the other constituencies that nominated me to thank them and tell them I would be running for election in another district, which I didn't yet want to announce. I was returning to Sverdlovsk because I could not tell my own people by telegram that I was declining their nomination.

My plan to run in Moscow and not in these constituencies

83

where I was sure to be elected was called a big mistake by both my opponents and my supporters—a crazy idea, sheer effrontery, overweening self-confidence. I had no answer to their criticism. My risk of losing was high, and I might be depriving myself of what was my only remaining chance of returning from political exile. Having overcome great obstacles placed in my way, I had now created a new obstacle for myself. No wonder it seemed strange to my critics.

Even so, I felt I had to run for the Moscow seat because it is the most important one in the country. I was not motivated by megalomania or conceit. I felt I had to prove both to myself and to those who supported me that a new time had come; that we were now able to decide our own fate; and that we could—despite all the pressure from the leadership, the apparat, and official ideology—go to the polling booth and make a real choice.

If I withdrew my candidacy in Moscow to run in Sverdlovsk, the need for an election campaign would virtually have disappeared right then and there. I would only have had to wait for election day, March 26. An overwhelming number of people in Sverdlovsk would undoubtedly have voted for me.

I estimated my chances in Moscow as being about fifty-fifty. My election campaign was like a continuation of the speech I made at the October 1987 meeting of the Central Committee. Then, I was alone, however, with the upper echelon of the party bureaucracy infuriated with me. The situation was quite different in my campaign: My opponents were the same bunch as before, only this time I was not on my own. The people of Moscow were on my side—and not only Muscovites. The majority of the country also detested the self-righteousness, hypocrisy, mendacity, condescending smugness, and conceit that riddles the entire structure of government.

I reached Sverdlovsk early in the morning. Although I

hadn't slept for a moment, being back home caused all the strain and fatigue of the past few days to vanish in a flash. I headed straight to a series of meetings with the people of Sverdlovsk. The first one lasted three hours. Then I went to another, at the Palace of Culture, where an audience of fifteen hundred handed up about five hundred written comments and questions. And on every other slip of paper the message was the same: "Boris Nikolayevich, give up the Moscow constituency; they'll make mincemeat of you—you can't trust Muscovites."

The meeting lasted until one o'clock in the morning. I explained to them the reasons I felt I had to run in Moscow. I think they understood me. They said that if I was not elected in Moscow I needn't worry; they would vote for *every* candidate on the Sverdlovsk list on election day, which would invalidate the vote; I might have a chance of running in the second election that would inevitably take place.

They obviously meant it, adding that on election day anyone who could would get a certificate removing his name from the electoral register in Sverdlovsk, fly to Moscow, and vote for me there as a "temporary resident," a procedure possible under the new electoral laws.

I had practically no time to sit and talk with any of my friends. Sadly, I had to leave. I was living at a crazy tempo then. It's not normal. There should always be time to spare for one's friends, but there was none. I went to see my mother. Lord, what she had had to endure in these last months! I embraced her quickly and left.

85

Tell us: Was it always your ambition to come to Moscow, or did it just happen?

How did you find a flat in Moscow?*

On April 3, 1985, my staff and I were sitting in the offices of the Sverdlovsk provincial committee, engaged in a heated discussion of problems regarding the spring planting season. We faced an emergency; very little snow had fallen that winter, resulting in a serious drought. The experts felt that we should wait before planting. We accepted that view, but we also decided to visit all the regions of the province and consult local experts. That evening I drove around to the food shops so I could see for myself how they were supplied. In general, things seemed to have improved; there were several kinds of

* Questions from the floor at meetings during the election campaign.

poultry for sale as well as cheese, eggs, and sausage, but even so the situation was less than satisfactory.

I never imagined that later that evening my thoughts would be several hundred miles away, following a call I received from Moscow offering me a position on the Central Committee as head of construction. I thought about it for a couple of seconds, then declined the offer.

I did not feel that I was ready for a position in Moscow. I had been born in Sverdlovsk, had studied and worked there, and still lived there. I liked my job, and although the changes I had brought about were small, they made a difference. But the main reason I declined was the relationships I had built up with local people—strong, enduring, worthwhile, the kind that take a long time to create.

Since most of all I was accustomed to working closely with people, it struck me as impossible to start fresh, leaving unfinished business in my hometown. There was another reason for my refusal. I wasn't fully aware of it at the time, but clearly it was lodged somewhere in my subconscious—namely, that it was not very logical for someone whose membership on the Central Committee was based on nine and a half years' service as first secretary of a provincial committee to be made section head of the Central Committee's construction department. Sverdlovsk province is the third largest in the country in terms of industrial production, and the first secretary of a province—possessing unique experience and knowledge—should be transferred to a post where he would be used to greater effect. Traditionally, this had always been the case: Kirilenko and Ryabev, both former provincial first secretaries, had been promoted to secretaries of the Central Committee. I was being offered the considerably more junior job of section head.

I continued to reflect on my future career practically all night, knowing that the phone call would not be the last I would hear of the matter. And it wasn't. The next day I was telephoned by Ligachev. Aware of my earlier conversation, he pressed even harder. Nevertheless, I stuck to my refusal, saying that I needed to stay where I was; that Sverdlovsk was an enormous, unique region of almost five million inhabitants, with many problems that were still unsolved, and therefore I could not leave. Then Ligachev used an irrefutable argument on me—party discipline, a Politburo decision— and said that as a Communist Party member, I was obligated to accept the proposal and move to Moscow.

There was no way around it; I would accept the position. On April 12, 1985, I started work in Moscow.

I was extremely sad to leave Sverdlovsk, where I had many good friends and comrades. My alma mater, the Urals Polytechnic Institute, was there too, and my work in the hard school of industry, from which I had switched to party work. There I had married, and there my two daughters were born and now a granddaughter as well. On top of it all, I was fifty-four years old—and changing my whole way of life and starting on a very different kind of job was very scary.

My reaction to moving to Moscow was typical of many people in my country. Attitudes toward Moscow are something unique. They manifest themselves, first, in a dislike of Muscovites—but this is combined with a passionate desire to move to Moscow and become a Muscovite. The reasons for these conflicting attitudes are understandable. They are formed by the strained social and economic conditions that exist in the USSR and from our age-old passion for creating Potemkin villages, intended to mask the hardships of those small towns. Moscow, which is visited by so many foreigners, is the one place that must look attractive on the surface. The food supply must always be tolerable. You could find in Moscow goods that were unavailable in the provinces for decades. As a result, provincials flock to Moscow, stand in lines for hours to buy imported shoes or sausages, and seethe with envy at the Muscovites, who are so lucky to have everything.

And the Muscovites, in their turn, curse the invading hordes because they pack the shops and make it impossible to buy anything. People in the provinces will do anything to send their grown-up children to Moscow, regardless of the humiliations and discomfort they may have to endure. A new word has even been coined, which until very recently was not to be found in any dictionary—*limitchik*. It refers to young men and women who live just beyond the Moscow city limits (hence the name) and who commute daily to the city, where they do mostly unskilled, menial work that, after a few years, will make them eligible to be given a Moscow residence permit and become legal residents of the city.

I must admit that I, too, used to have a prejudiced attitude toward Muscovites. When I was living in Sverdlovsk and had to make frequent business trips to the capital, I never had much opportunity to meet the people of Moscow socially. For the most part, I came in contact with politicians and officials at the republic and national level, but even these encounters tended to leave a nasty taste in my mouth. No one made any attempt to hide his or her attitude of snobbery and arrogance toward provincials, and my reaction was to assume that all Muscovites behaved like that.

Furthermore, I did not have any ambition to work in Moscow. I had turned down offers of jobs there, even the post of minister. I have always loved Sverdlovsk; I still love it and have never regarded it as provincial. I don't think these feelings diminish me in any way.

But now I was in Moscow. I was shown an apartment, and because I was feeling so depressed I didn't really care what sort of place it was. I accepted what was offered—in a noisy, dirty part of town, quite distant from the leaders of our party, who usually live in the outer suburb of Kuntsevo, where it is quiet, clean, and comfortable.

I plunged into my job at a furious pace, and the construction section started to come to life. Not everyone could keep up with me, but that was natural. I would come home every evening around midnight, and by eight o'clock the next morning I was at work again. I did not demand that others work those hours, but some colleagues, especially my deputies, did their best to keep up.

I never felt any kind of awe when I crossed the threshold of the Central Committee's building on Moscow's Staraya Square. The building is, in reality, the real citadel of power in the USSR, the place where the might of the party's apparat is concentrated. Proposals, orders, and appointments are generated there, as well as a stream of grandiose but unrealizable programs, relentlessly upbeat slogans, dubious schemes, and straight crimes. Decisions like the one to send troops to Afghanistan have been made there in minutes.

I started work without giving a thought to such matters. The section had to be put into working condition. I was very familiar with the problems of the construction industry—as a manager in disguise, I knew all about the chief difficulties and problems of that sector of the economy.

I had been fortunate that until Moscow I had practically never had to work as a subordinate. I had been a section manager but never an assistant manager; managing director but never the deputy managing director of a trust. Never having been a number two, I was used to making decisions without shifting the ultimate responsibility onto someone else. In the Central Committee, however, the structure of subordination, of a strict party hierarchy, has been taken to the point of absurdity—everything is hedged with precautionary reservations, every proposal needs some superior figure's approval. Working within such a frigidly bureaucratic framework was an ordeal for someone of my freewheeling and self-confident temperament. The construction section was subordinate to Vladimir Dolgikh, and he was one of the first persons to come in conflict with my independent style of work.

At the first meeting of section heads that I attended, Dolgikh made a speech. I noticed that everyone else had come prepared with a thick notebook, and they were all scribbling away, recording every word. I listened intently and noted only the main points, in single-word headings. Dolgikh, evidently accustomed to his practically every word being written down, kept glancing at me with obvious displeasure and an expression that implied: "What is this? I am uttering pearls of wisdom, and you are not writing them down!" Although he said nothing at the time, on the next occasion he made a point of asking me, "Have you any questions? Perhaps there is something you don't remember. If so, ask me." "No," I replied. "I've remembered everything." Because he knew that my current position was temporary and that my status might be abruptly changed, I never in fact had any conflicts or problems in my relations with him.

There was an overwhelming amount of work to be done in my department. I do not regret my time in that section, though, because there were rewards. I got to know the state of affairs in the country as a whole, and I kept in touch with the republics and several of the biggest provinces. I also had dealings with Gorbachev—who by now had become general secretary—but only by telephone. I must say I was amazed that he did not try to meet me, because we did have a good personal relationship. He also knew that like me, he had moved up to the Central Committee from the position of regional first secretary—and from a region that was considerably inferior to Sverdlovsk in economic potential. But *he* had been promoted to the rank of general secretary of the Central Committee. I think Gorbachev knew this was on my mind, but neither of us gave any sign of it.

After a while my wife joined me, with my older daughter, her husband, and my little granddaughters. (My younger daughter was already living in Moscow.) They made the apartment livable while I worked.

92

Before I continue my story about my career in industry and party work, I would like to say something about the people who are closest to me. My family consists of my wife, my two daughters and their husbands, my two granddaughters, and a grandson. The newcomers did not find it easy in Moscow: an unfamiliar city, a new tempo of life, new relationships. Usually the head of the family helps the others find their feet, but I had neither the energy nor the time to keep track of how things were going at home; I was totally absorbed in my work, with the result that, if anything, I saw less of my family in Moscow than in Sverdlovsk.

But let me begin at the beginning—which means going back to my days at the polytechnic in the 1950s.

In the whirlpool of student life, a group of us formed a clique of our own—six boys and six girls. We lived near each other, in two large rooms of a student dormitory, and we would meet nearly every evening. Inevitably boys and girls fell in love with each other, and I, too, was attracted to some of the girls. Gradually, though, in that large, friendly student family, I began to pay more and more attention to one girl in particular—Naya Girina. She had been born in Orenburg province and was officially named Anastasia, but her parents and everyone else called her Naya. The name has stuck, so much so that she is seldom called by her given name.

When she was very young this was not a problem, but when she started work and people began calling her by her first name and patronymic, she found it difficult to answer to the formal names. Perhaps she ought to have accustomed herself to it, but instead she went to the records office and had her name changed to Naya. I prefer Anastasia, and for a long time I didn't address her by any name but affectionately called her Devushka, meaning "girl."

She has always been a modest, charming, and gentle person. These characteristics are a necessary contrast to my extroverted nature. Our feelings for each other grew gradually, but we gave each other no sign. Whenever I kissed her, it was on the cheek, as with all the other girls, and we did not make any passionate declarations. Our platonic relationship lasted for a long time, although inwardly I realized that I had fallen for her, fallen hard, in fact, and there was no getting away from it. It wasn't until our second year that we admitted we loved each other. We were standing behind the pillars in the upstairs gallery, at the entrance to the institute's assembly hall. We kissed—this time not on the cheek but for real.

In our final year at the polytechnic, I was away for a few months playing volleyball, and when I returned I plunged furiously into work on my dissertation. After I passed the final exams, I went away on tour with the team again, without even bothering to find out where I had been assigned for my first job. When I got back I learned that I was to stay in Sverdlovsk and Naya was being sent to Orenburg. Young couples are assigned to the same town only when they are married. All that we had was our pledge that we loved each other. Instead of marrying right away, we decided to test our love and see how strong and deep it was.

We agreed that she would go to Orenburg and I would stay in Sverdlovsk, and that after exactly one year we would meet on neutral ground. We would find out for certain whether our feelings for each other had cooled or had grown even warmer and stronger. That is what we did.

I have already described how much strain I was under during that year—the year in which I put myself through the process of learning the twelve basic manual trades in the construction industry while continuing to play on the city volleyball team. By coincidence, exactly a year later the regional volleyball tournament took place in Kuibyshev. Naya and I spoke on the telephone. She was very excited; so much so, in fact, that I hardly recognized her voice. I was also very ex-

94

cited, my mood even more elated than hers. We arranged a time to meet in the town square.

Our team's hotel was in the square. Sure enough, as I came out of the hotel, I saw her. My heart was ready to burst with a flood of emotions; I looked at her, and I knew at once that we would spend the rest of our lives together. All that night we walked around the town together, talking about everything under the sun. We recalled our student days and told each other everything that had happened over the past year. I just wanted to go on listening and listening to her, to go on looking at her day and night.

Our lives have proved that we were brought together by fate. Naya took me and loved me as I am—obstinate and prickly—and I confess she has not had an easy time with me. As for myself, I need hardly say that I have always loved her —and will love her all my life.

We went back to Sverdlovsk and gathered our friends from the polytechnic at the hostel where I was living and told them that we had decided to get married. In those days, you did not have to give advance notice of your intention to marry; you just turned up at the marriage bureau with your witnesses, the registrar conducted the ceremony, you signed the book and went home.

During my time at the polytechnic, particularly in the last year or two, when there were a lot of marriages, I was one of the chief organizers of the so-called Komsomol weddings— noisy, cheerful occasions with lots of ingenious impromptu entertainment. Thus I was, in a way, present at the start of many families. Now all my friends got together and arranged a splendid Komsomol wedding for us.

Our friends arrived from all over the country, since many of them were already working in other towns. It was a magnificent wedding reception, with about 150 guests. The boys thought up a number of entertainments and did everything to ensure that we would remember our wedding for the rest of our lives. They composed an ode to us, presented us with a hilarious homemade newspaper, and offered other delightfully funny surprises.

The reception lasted all night. But that was not to be the end of it: My relatives demanded a second wedding reception, since there had not been room for everyone at the first one and the guests had largely been young people. So we arranged another reception for our relations. Then we went to Orenburg, where Naya's family demanded yet a third reception. She comes from a genuine peasant family, where old traditions are still observed. The reception, for about thirty people, was held in their own small home. Afterward we were taken next door, to spend the night in a neighbor's house. We had barely wakened the next morning when we heard people outside shouting, "Show us the sheet!" According to ancient custom, on the morning after the wedding night, the couple must hang their sheet out the window, where it can be seen from the street. This, however, was our third "wedding," so we had to go out on the porch and give a frank account of ourselves to the crowd who had gathered there.

We stayed with Naya's parents for several days; in the evenings we would sit on the porch, looking out over a large meadow, and talk and dream of the future, of what our life would be.

When we returned to Sverdlovsk, Naya started working at the Institute of Waterways, where she remained for twenty-nine years, becoming chief engineer of a large project. Slightly less than a year later, we had our first child, a baby girl. Though I'd wanted a son, I was delighted, and we named her Lena. My friends and I gathered outside the clinic and threw flowers through Naya's window. Then we returned home and marked the occasion with a dinner. A little over two years later, I took Naya to the maternity clinic again. I had followed all the customs prescribed by people who know about such things—including putting an ax and a man's peaked cap under the pillow. Friends assured me that now my wife was certain to have a boy. None of the tried-and-true devices worked, however, and we had another daughter—Tanya. She was a gentle, smiling baby, who took after her mother. Lena is more like me.

I must confess that I don't remember too many details of their childhood—such as when they started to walk and talk, or the rare moments when I tried to help raise them. I was working almost around the clock, and we would all meet only on Sunday afternoons, when we had a big family lunch together. When my daughters were a little older, we would plan our family parties in a restaurant they loved. The Great Urals restaurant was never very full in the daytime, and there we would order lunch—always with ice cream for dessert, an event of particular importance to Lena and Tanya.

My daughters have always treated me affectionately and tenderly; they have always wanted to please me. When they were in school, I was never able to attend the parent-teacher meetings, but both girls did well, always getting top grades. I had told them at the start that 80 was not a mark worth getting. They worked hard, and they were easy to raise. There were the usual problems, from which everyone suffers—their wanting something they could not have or the sleepless nights when one of them was ill—but that is normal.

For as long as we have been married, my wife and I have spent our vacations together, except once when I went alone to Kisovodsk, a spa in the north Caucasus. We felt that the girls were still too young to take with us, so Naya decided to stay at home with them. But within days I sent her a telegram: "Come at once. Can't stand it." Naya found someone to look after the girls and flew south to join me. We rented a private apartment and once more took our holiday together. Beginning when our daughters were six and eight, all four of us would camp in a forest by the edge of a lake.

When the children were older, we took a steamer trip down the Kama and Volga rivers, stopping in Gelendzhika, where we set up a whole village of tents. To this day, I remember those holidays we spent in the wild, like savages. There was nothing but laughter from morning till night, for we kept inventing funny games and quizzes and playing practical jokes. Those were real vacations, when one could totally relax—quite unlike the holidays I have now, when from almost the first day of my leave I can't stop thinking about work. Nowadays people say that I seldom smile; perhaps this is true, although I am by nature an optimist.

After primary school, Lena went to the Urals Polytechnic, where, following in her father's footsteps, she graduated from the faculty of civil engineering. She now works at an exhibition of construction technology and methods. Tanya was interested in mathematics and cybernetics, and she attended Moscow University to study those subjects. I did not try to dissuade her from going to Moscow, although my wife didn't like the idea at all. She would weep, convinced that Tanya would find living alone in Moscow very difficult. Our daughter, despite her gentle nature, proved to be very insistent and got her way. I often went to Moscow on business, so we still saw a lot of each other. After graduation she stayed in Moscow for her first job. She now works with very powerful computers; she is responsible for programming and for solving complex problems. This is the kind of job she wanted, and I think it satisfies her.

Lena met and married Valery Okulov, an aircraft navigator based in Sverdlovsk. Tanya's husband is Lyosha Dyachenko. Both sons-in-law are good fellows, and although they have never called me "father," I regard my daughters' husbands as my children too. We are all together now, one big family, living in Moscow. Both my daughters' marriages are excellent, based on kindness and mutual respect. They are, I think, enviable relationships. Lena was the first to have a child, Katya, and make me a grandfather. Then Tanya had a boy she named Boris. I am very grateful that he was named after me; now there are two Boris Yeltsins in the world.

Lena has since had another baby, Mashenka, who is a sweet, placid, happy child. Katya is different: lively, restless, and bright. Young Boris is very energetic; he took up sports at an early age—playing tennis when only seven.

We share an apartment with Tanya and her family. Lena and her family live near us and often come to visit and dine with us. Because I always get home late, we can have family gatherings only on Sundays. For me that is a real occasion. They are all concerned about me and very attentive, especially since I am always being bothered by my work. I am constantly having a fight with someone, and I often have sleepless nights. Their sympathy and support for my problems have always helped me survive my most difficult moments.

At the plenum in June 1985, I was elected secretary of the Central Committee responsible for the construction industry. To be honest, I felt no particular pleasure about this promotion. I considered it to be a natural progression. It was at last a real job, which measured up to my abilities and experience. Now I would see how the leaders of government lived in our country.

As a section chief, I had been allowed a small weekend dacha in the country (shared with another family), but now, as head of a department of the Central Committee, I was offered the dacha that Gorbachev had moved out of when a new one was built especially for him.

I made plans for trips to various republics and provinces— to the provinces of Moscow and Leningrad, to the Far East, to Turkmenia, Armenia, Tyumen province in Siberia, and other parts of the country. I also made a memorable trip to Tashkent for a plenum of the Central Committee of the Communist Party of Uzbekistan. A lot of people in the city had heard of my arrival, and they gathered outside my hotel, demanding that they be allowed in to talk to me. The authorities, of course, began to chase them away, but I said that over the next two days I would see anyone who asked for an interview. And I asked my bodyguard to make sure that all those wishing to talk to me were let in.

The first person to come was a member of the KGB, who told me about the appalling level of bribery that flourished in Uzbekistan. He said that after Sharaf Rashidov had been dismissed for gross corruption from his post as first secretary of the Uzbek Communist Party, nothing had really changed. Usmankhodzhaev, the new secretary, was taking as many bribes as his predecessor. This KGB official brought a number of documents with him containing serious evidence against Usmankhodzhaev. He asked for my help. Only Moscow could do what was necessary, he said; here the least attempt to take any sort of action met the resistance of a corrupt bureaucracy. I promised to read the documents carefully, and if what they revealed was really serious, I would report on the matter at the highest level.

He was followed by an endless stream of visitors, who kept on coming for the entire two days. I listened to what seemed totally improbable but were in fact entirely real stories of bribery in the upper echelons of the Uzbek Communist Party.

From all these stories there emerged a system of corruption of officials from top to bottom. An honest person needed real courage not to get caught up in the chain of bribery. It was mostly these honest people who had come to see me. I resolved to tell Gorbachev about it as soon as I returned to Moscow.

On this trip, another event occurred that was symptomatic. I asked for the bill for the food and drink I had consumed in the hotel and, to my amazement, was told that it had already been taken care of. I insisted to my hosts that I be responsible for my bill, but I found that my food and drink had been paid for out of a special fund of the Central Committee of the Uzbekistan. Unable to restrain myself, almost shouting, I demanded my bill and paid it myself.

On the flight back to Moscow I carefully studied all the documents given to me by the KGB official. Then I went to see Gorbachev and gave him a detailed account of everything I had found out, advising him that firm action should be taken immediately, and above all that the accusations against Usmankhodzhaev must be investigated. Unexpectedly, Gorbachev lost his temper. He told me that I knew nothing about these matters, that Usmankhodzhaev was an honest Communist, and that because he had had to wage a campaign against Rashidov's reign of corruption, the old mafia was trying to compromise him with false denunciations and slanderous rumors. I countered by repeating that I was only just back from Tashkent, and that Usmankhodzhaev had simply taken over Rashidov's system and was lining his pockets by utilizing a machinery of corruption he didn't even create himself. Gorbachev replied that I had been fooled, and that anyway Ligachev had personally vouched for Usmankhodzhaev. I had no answer to that; the fact that he had been given a clean bill of health by the number two man in the whole party (as Ligachev was then) was a serious matter. Before leaving, I asked Gorbachev to take a closer look at this serious matter. After my resignation from the Politburo and the Central Committee, Usmankhodzhaev was sacked from his job, arrested, tried, and convicted.

But I have gotten ahead of my story. Those events were to happen later. Then I was working as a secretary of the Central Committee and was trying to draw up a realistic program that might help the construction industry get out of a crisis. I did not suspect that my fate was already decided. The telephone rang in my office. I was ordered to go to the Politburo at once.

5

March 6, 1989

Chronicle of the Election Campaign

As I watched my enemies make one mistake after another in their fight against me, I used to wonder what I would do if I were put in charge of a campaign to undermine Yeltsin as a candidate for people's deputy. I know what stupid errors I would *not* make. To start with, I would remove the mystery from the name Yeltsin. He would be treated as just another ordinary candidate, like Ivanov or Petrov. I would immediately allow—no, I would *force*—every newspaper and magazine to interview him at least twice a month. In no time everyone would be bored to death with Yeltsin. And I would make sure that he was seen on television often, on every suitable—and unsuitable—program. Before too long the electorate would be absolutely fed up with hearing his thoughts and ideas. *Then* I might have a chance of sabotaging the election chances of the undesirable Yeltsin.

Instead, everything that has been done has given me a martyr's halo, which gets brighter every day. The official press has kept silent about me, and the only interviews with me are those broadcast by Western radio stations. Every new move against me only makes the Moscow voters more and more indignant; and since there have been a lot of such moves, the result is that my enemies have sabotaged their own efforts and ensured that Yeltsin be elected deputy for the Moscow number 1 constituency.

So obvious are the mistakes that people ask whether in fact Lev Zaikov, my enemy and successor as first secretary of the Moscow City Committee of the Party, is not perhaps my secret supporter. Everyone advises me that when the voting is over and I have been elected, I must be sure to telephone Zaikov and thank him for the "enormous help and support" that he has given me during the election campaign. Total ignorance of the laws of human behavior and a complete inability to gauge people's reactions have invariably led my enemies to achieve the exact opposite of what they intended.

Western correspondents have often asked whether I have worked out any particular tactics in my election campaign, or whether I have any secrets that may secure my hoped-for victory at the polls. Simpleminded though it may sound, I have had only one tactical weapon in the campaign—common sense. In practice, this means never doing or saying anything that might insult or denigrate my opponent, Brakov. On campaign swings and at meetings, I only tell the truth, however uncomfortable or detrimental it may be; I strive to be utterly frank and, most important of all, always to sense people's thoughts and feelings.

Almost every day I held meetings with huge groups of people, and during the last month before the election I attended two such meetings daily. This was exhausting, but they filled me with confidence. Though winning was my personal objective, I was beginning to feel sure that with people like these, who had such a genuine hunger to see justice and good done, we were bound, in spite of everything, to haul ourselves out of the situation in which we found ourselves.

I liked large organized meetings much less, especially those with audiences of several thousand. There were occasions where as many as a hundred thousand people gathered in Moscow's Luzhniki stadium. In those conditions you can't make out individual faces or see people's eyes. But such meetings are certainly the best lessons for politicians. There one has to seize the attention of a vast mass of people with words alone; one false word and you can be driven from the rostrum.

I regret that Gorbachev never participates in such large meetings. I believe he would find it very useful. Accustomed as he is to talking to specially prepared, selected people, brought in by the busload to represent the toiling masses, the experience of addressing those meetings at Luzhniki would be a most valuable lesson for him. Perhaps one of these days he will actually do it.

Mass meetings can be dangerous weapons in a political battle. People don't restrain their emotions, and they don't use parliamentary language. Consequently, a speech made at such a meeting must be precisely worded and all the more carefully calculated in advance. It is hard for me to be exact, but I have probably taken part in as many as twenty large meetings, each one attended by several thousand people. Complex feelings are aroused when a huge mass of people catch sight of you and rhythmically chant, "Yeltsin, Yeltsin!" Men, women, young, old . . . To be honest, I feel no pleasure or elation at such moments. One has to go up to the rostrum as quickly as possible, take the microphone, and start to speak, in order to calm that wave of excitement and euphoria. When people start listening, the atmosphere changes. I regard such enthusiasm with a certain inner caution, because we all know only too well how easily people can be thrilled and, equally, can easily lose faith in you. For that reason it is better not to fall prey to any false illusions. After these meetings I would get into arguments with my trusted supporters, who believed that the louder people chanted my name, the greater the success of the meeting. That is nonsense.

But my campaign workers and supporters deserve enormous credit. I shall always be grateful to them for their selfless support, their sincerity, devotion, and loyalty. Many people said that I was making a terrible mistake choosing people who were not professionals as my campaign aides—not politicians, not experts, but plain, intelligent, decent human beings. I knew none of them before the election campaign started; they either phoned or came to see me, saying that they wanted to work as my campaign assistants. I was grateful for this but warned them that it would be extremely tough going. They knew this, of course, but they were dedicated and worked night and day. They are all wonderful people.

What were the shortcomings in your work as first secretary of the Moscow City Committee? Was authoritarianism one of them?

Is it true that at your first meeting with the people of Moscow you received letters from party mafiosi and their wives, promising to "rip the feeble sails of *perestroika* to shreds"? *

On December 22, 1985, I was summoned to the Politburo. I did not know why I had been called, but when I saw that there were no Central Committee secretaries but only members of the Politburo, I realized that the subject of the meeting was myself. Gorbachev began by saying that the Politburo had discussed the matter and decided that I, Yeltsin, should take over as head of the Moscow City Committee of

---

* Questions from the floor at meetings during the election campaign.

the Communist Party—an organization of almost 1,200,000 members. This was totally unexpected. I stood up and expressed my doubts about whether I was the right person for the job. First of all, I was a civil engineer and had worked much of my life in the construction industry. I still had a number of unfinished projects for getting the department out of the blind alley in which it found itself. I felt that I would be more useful if I continued my work as a secretary of the Central Committee. Furthermore, I knew very few people in the Moscow party organization, and I would find the job very difficult.

Gorbachev and the other Politburo members tried to persuade me that my appointment was essential; that Viktor Grishin, the incumbent, had to be replaced; that the Moscow party organization was in a state of utter decline; that its working style and methods were such that not only did it not set a good example but it was in fact less effective than the other party organizations in the country. Grishin, they declared, gave no thought to people and their pressing needs. He had let the work slide, being concerned only with outward show and with putting on spectacular public events—noisy and carefully rehearsed, the kind of events where everyone read their lines from prepared scripts. The Politburo felt strongly that the Moscow party organization was in need of a rescue operation.

The discussion in the Politburo turned out to be difficult, at times embarrassing. Again I was told that I was subject to party discipline; that they believed I would be more useful to the party in Moscow. Finally, after forcing myself to admit that the Moscow party organization certainly couldn't be left in its present state, and after suggesting the names of other people who might be given the job, I accepted the appointment.

I have often wondered how Gorbachev chose me for the job. He must have taken into account my ten years of experience in Sverdlovsk leading one of the largest party organizations in the country, as well as my experience in industry. Furthermore, he knew my character and must have felt certain I would be able to clear away the old debris, to fight the mafia, and he knew that I was tough enough to carry out a wholesale cleanup of all the personnel. All this had been decided in advance. I suppose I really was the most suitable candidate at the time for the purposes he had in mind, but I still had misgivings. Not because I was afraid of the difficulties ahead, but because I realized that I was being used as the means of pushing Grishin out of the job. He was a man of no great intellect, and he lacked any sense of moral decency. He was a mixture of bombast and servility; he knew, at any moment, exactly what needed to be done in order to curry favor with the leadership. Possessing an extremely high opinion of himself, he was laying plans to get himself eventually made general secretary and was trying to do everything possible to prepare himself to take power. Luckily, he was prevented from doing so.

He had corrupted many people in the Moscow City Committee leadership, although fortunately not the whole Moscow party organization. The ill effects of his term were manifested in public affairs, in the people's standard of living, and in Moscow's outward appearance. Because of him, life in the capital was worse than it had been several decades before: dirt, endless lines, overcrowded public transportation.

Gorbachev spoke on December 24 at a plenum of the Moscow City Committee. Grishin was dismissed—"retired at his own request, as he was of pensionable age," the classic phrase for putting an unwanted politician out to pasture. I was proposed as his successor, which surprised no one and evoked no questions. I expressed my gratitude for the party's confidence in me, adding that I promised them nothing but hard work. The plenum then took its otherwise uneventful course.

A conference of the Moscow party organization, to hear

reports and elect new officials, was set for the following February, and I suspected that the main battle would take place then. Grishin's "old guard" would try to reverse the course of events.

I had to concentrate on preparing for that conference. As research for my report, I met with dozens of people, visited enterprises all over the city in order to analyze their problems, and, in consultation with specialists, tried to find the best way out of the state of crisis. My report to the conference lasted two hours. When I had finished, Gorbachev said, "You have brought in a strong and welcome gust of fresh air," although he said it without an approving smile and with an impassive expression.

We had to rebuild practically from zero. The first task was to change the staff of the City Committee's bureau, since it was full of Grishin's cronies. Grishin had long since become ineffective. In truth, he had never had any real authority, and now that *perestroika* was gathering momentum, his presence in the Politburo compromised the party's highest decision-making body. Gorbachev never acts decisively, and in Grishin's case, too, he procrastinated. The man should have been fired much earlier. When I started tackling the mess in Moscow, Grishin outwardly raised no objections. I was told that he was indignant over some of the things I did, but that was only talk; he never made any specific moves to cause me trouble.

Attempts were made to incriminate him in various corrupt operations, but the law enforcement officials were never able to discover any solid evidence against him. I was told that it must have been destroyed. I do not rule out that possibility, because we could not even find the documents recording his entry into the party, and these must once have existed. The mass of rumors about Grishin were never confirmed. I know that when I took over his job, his office safes were empty. If there was evidence against him at KGB headquarters, I simply don't know of it.

I guessed he would try to block me sooner or later, especially in the matter of personnel changes, and indeed he did try to do this, by having other people recommend "his" man as chairman of the executive committee of the Moscow Soviet. Every time a key post came open, I always wondered whether one of Grishin's men would be eased into the job, and I took certain steps to prevent any possibility of this happening. The permanent staff of the City Committee, especially those people who had worked for a long time under Grishin, had to be replaced. These apparatchiks were infected with all the vices of the Brezhnev era: toadyism, servility, and boot-licking, attitudes that had become thoroughly ingrained. There was no way to reeducate these people. They simply had to be dismissed and replaced. And this I did.

My assistants—inherited from Grishin—I fired at once, while the staffs of the bureau and the City Committee were dismissed slowly but surely. I looked for people to replace them. Vasily Zakharov was recommended to me at the Central Committee as second secretary; he had recently been working in the science department of the Central Committee and before that he was secretary of the Leningrad Committee of the Party.

The incumbent chairman of the executive committee of the Moscow Soviet was Promyslov, a man notorious not only to Muscovites. A joke about him used to circulate: "Promyslov made a short stopover in Moscow while flying from Washington to Tokyo."

Promyslov came to see me the day after my election, and while standing in the doorway of my office, he began to tell me how impossible it had been to work under Grishin, then made several more unflattering remarks about him. Without drawing breath, he went on to say how glad he was that I was now first secretary. Finally he announced that he had miraculously got his second wind; he was full of energy, which would undoubtedly last for at least another five years. I stopped him and declared that the news I had for him was rather different. I said harshly that he was to be retired—but decently, at his own request. I asked him to bring his resignation at noon the next day. I urged him not to be late. When he did not come at the appointed hour, I phoned him and mentioned that he obviously had not heard what I had said: I had proposed that he be retired "decently," but there were, of course, other ways of doing it. He understood, and twenty minutes later he brought me his letter of resignation.

Over the next two days, four groups of people proposed four different candidates for the post of chairman of the Moscow Soviet. Each group, I realized, was pushing its own man. Everyone knows what an important figure the chairman of the city soviet is—he is the mayor of the city, and much depends on him. I decided to use an unconventional method of selection. I went to the ZIL automobile factory, where I stayed from 8 A.M. until 2 A.M. the following morning. I walked around the workshops, met workers, specialists, active party members, designers, and section foremen. But that was only one part of my visit. I also got acquainted with Valery Saikin, the general manager. As I toured the factory with him, I paid attention to everything: how he talked to the workers, to the secretary of the party committee, to me. After a few days, I decided he would make a good chairman of the city soviet; not immediately, of course, as he would need help and support while he worked himself into this new and very different job. I discussed my idea with Gorbachev. He approved of it, and although Saikin did not accept at once, he agreed after giving it some thought to take on the post. I continued my shake-up of the City Committee by replacing all the secretaries.

I then made a visit to the editorial offices of the newspaper

Moscow Pravda, where I met the entire staff and talked frankly with them for more than four hours. The newspaper had just acquired a new editor in chief, Mikhail Poltoranin, who had previously worked on *Pravda*, the official national newspaper. This honest and talented journalist had immediately changed the atmosphere of the Moscow paper and published articles that alarmed and frightened many people. I remember, for instance, a story titled "Carriages at the Door," which concerned the misuse of official cars by party and government functionaries. The article, which created a big stir in Moscow at the time, was not only hard-hitting; I would say it was very daring for those days. Poltoranin was thereupon summoned to the Central Committee to be criticized, but before going he telephoned to ask me what I thought of the article. I said I thought it was perfectly acceptable. An equally stormy reaction was produced by the publication in *Moscow Komsomol* of stories on drug addiction, prostitution, and organized crime—subjects about which nothing had ever been written before. In general, Moscow's city newspapers had stopped being discreet and obedient. I welcomed this openness, and when people tried to persuade me that it was a bad thing to be so critical and to expose Moscow's problems—because it was the capital and the country's shop window—I responded by asking whether or not these negative phenomena existed. On being assured that they did, I suggested that by concealing the sore points we were not healing them but merely covering them up with sweet-smelling cream so they wouldn't be visible. Any such social evils must be brought out into the open, however painful this might be.

I also had several meetings with Moscow television production staffs. They had just moved into new offices, and a new editor of news and current affairs had been appointed. A number of interesting programs were beginning to appear, especially "Moscow and the Muscovites" and "Good Evening, Moscow." Moscow's television was becoming much livelier.

As might be expected, the new-style Moscow press and television very soon produced a strongly negative reaction. I have already spoken of Poltoranin's summons before the Central Committee; this happened a number of times. One day he was kept waiting outside the office of a highly placed bureaucrat—disgraceful behavior. I defended him in every way I could. People kept complaining to Gorbachev, and one day, during a session of the Politburo, he said to me, "He's done it again, your Poltoranin!" To which I replied, "Our Poltoranin runs a good newspaper; its circulation is going up all the time. You'd do better to keep your eye on Yuri Afanasiev," referring to the editor of *Pravda*. At that time subscriptions to *Pravda* were falling off, despite the fact that every member of the Communist Party was obliged to subscribe.

When I was dismissed from my job as first secretary of the Moscow party organization in 1988, it became obvious that Poltoranin would not last much longer, and indeed he was very soon replaced. But that was later.

I continued to fight on Moscow's behalf. Absolutely everything was in a state of neglect. The city had fallen behind in practically all the targets that had been set in the 1972 general plan for its development. Seven hundred thousand workers had migrated to the city from all over the country, and the actual population of Moscow exceeded the projected figure by 1,100,000. Added to that, short-term visitors numbered about three million a month in summer, two million in winter, and no provision had been made for them. The result was a desperate picture we could all see with our own eyes: more lines and dirt, the metro and surface transportation all overcrowded. The city was bursting at the seams, and the situation in Moscow's cultural life was equally bad. For instance, the number of theater seats per thousand inhabitants was actually less than in 1917.

During the first year of my time in office in Moscow, the secretaries of the Central Committee and the members of the Politburo did try to help, especially since Gorbachev kept urging them to do so. In those early months, I conceived the idea of organizing fairs, not one-time events but permanent features of the city and a constant source of enjoyment for both Muscovites and visitors. Booths and amusement parks were set up on empty lots, and contracts were signed directly with other cities and republics to supply fruits and vegetables. Not all of the fairs were successful, but in many districts they became pleasant places for family outings. This was important because Moscow lacked public events and places for simple, inexpensive entertainment. The fairs have lived on to this day, and Muscovites have grown to count on them. They regard them as their own creation and could now hardly imagine life without them.

I also introduced several traditions that I had established in Sverdlovsk. I had meetings with a number of citizens' groups, one of the first being with about two thousand people who communicated information and propaganda to the public on behalf of the party. I spoke to them in the great hall of the House of Political Education, and then I offered to answer any questions—even the most hostile—that people wanted to ask. And there were a few hostile ones, such as this foreboding warning: "You, Yeltsin, have started to tackle the Moscow mafia. We've been through this before—Khrushchev wanted to pack all of us off to labor camps. If you go on the way you have, someone else will have your job in two years' time." Ironically, this prediction came true. It may have been pure coincidence, but two years later I was dismissed, although I don't think the mafia had anything to do with it.

But while I was first secretary I discovered instances of the mafia at work. I began receiving a number of letters denouncing bribery and corruption in the retail trade and in the police. They were investigated, but the investigators either could not or would not expose the system. The investigative departments of the Ministry of Internal Affairs (which was responsible for the police) and the Moscow division of the KGB were called in to help, as were the newly appointed heads of the retail network and the organization responsible for Moscow's restaurants. We began replacing management personnel, but we still could not penetrate the closed circle.

Yet more and more facts accumulated; people saw things and wrote to us about them, but mainly anonymously. For instance, complaints about bribery and theft at a particular chain of butcher shops began to accumulate, involving the inflation of the number of slaughtered animals. It was all happening under the protection of the first secretary of a certain district. As a result, the matter came up for discussion in the City Committee.

Learning one day that a certain butcher shop had received a delivery of veal, I went and stood in line. Because it was still the start of my term, not many people knew my face. When my turn came at the counter, I asked for a kilo of veal. A clerk replied that there was beef but no veal. I said that was not true and asked to see the manager. One or two people in line realized who I was and started making a scene. I insisted on being taken to the back of the shop, and there I found the veal, which was being loaded onto a truck. There was an almighty fuss, and the management was fired.

A second incident came up when I was visiting a factory cafeteria. I asked why there were no carrots and was told that none had been delivered. With the help of the managers, I checked out the story. The porters who unloaded the supplies told us that the carrots had indeed been delivered, but they had been spirited away to an unknown destination the same day. The documents that might have confirmed the delivery had conveniently vanished. It was a very efficient cover-up.

And there was corruption in the manager's office of a grocery store, where mystery surrounded a large quantity of packages containing various delicacies. When I asked whom they were for, I was told they were outside orders awaiting delivery. I was greeted with silence when I asked if anyone could place an order. Then we began to question the manager, and she admitted that the orders were distributed according to rank to officials of the district executive committee of the soviet, the Ministry of Foreign Affairs, the district committee of the party, and municipal offices. When I examined the city's balance sheet for a number of grocery and delicatessen foods, I discovered a strange discrepancy. According to official statistics, several more tons of each item were brought into the city than were eaten, even accounting for normal waste. As a rule, no one comes forward to reveal the workings of the system. But I did have a stroke of luck. By now many people knew that I often went into shops, markets, and warehouses; they knew what I was looking for but were clearly afraid to come forward. Then one day as I walked out of a shop, a young woman came up to me in the street. She said that she had something of the greatest importance to tell me. There and then I set the day and time for her to come to see me in my office at the City Committee.

To this day I feel indignation when I recall her story of bribes and kickbacks. She had only recently been drawn into the system and was unable to stand it. The scheme was amazingly well thought out. Each salesperson was obliged to overcharge the customer and hand a certain sum each day to his or her supervisor, who kept part of it for himself and gave part to the general manager of the store. Then the money was shared out among the management, from top to bottom. The staff at the warehouse also got kickbacks according to a predetermined scale. Every employee knew two or three people in the chain. In the wholesale trade there was another, much bigger, scale of kickbacks.

The young woman was extremely frightened and begged to

be protected. I did all I could to ensure that she was not recognized and victimized; she was soon transferred to another shop. I called together my inner circle, and we decided to carry out a program of dismissal and replacement: We would fine not just individual culprits but the managerial staff of whole sectors of the retail trade, whole departments, and whole sections of the work force at warehouses. We would replace them with young, "uninfected" staff. In a period of just over a year, about eight hundred people were tried and convicted of criminal offenses.

But that was only part of the mafia. We were never able to get our hands on the really big operators in the "black economy," which represents up to 15 percent of the gross volume of goods in the retail network of the country. Neither could we touch the top end of the mafia, with its links to politicians. We did not have enough time. My term of two years came to an end, and in retrospect it is my impression that the Moscow City Committee subsequently lost much of its zeal for tackling this problem.

But I did make headway in some areas. Of the thirty-three first secretaries of district committees, twenty-three were replaced. Some were promoted; others were obliged to leave after a frank, tough talk, either with me or with the bureau of the City Committee or at a plenum of the district committee. Most of them conceded they were unable to work in the new way. But some had to be persuaded, and it was an unpleasant, painful process.

Their replacements were not always well chosen. It turned out that we had made several unsatisfactory appointments of people who failed to improve the style of work and the state of affairs in their districts. This happened, first, because I didn't know the Moscow party well enough, and, second, because of the faulty practice of selecting people for jobs purely on the basis of the questionnaires they filled out and their previous positions. Essentially, that meant that we were promoting not the person but his or her résumé, and consequently mistakes were made.

I was later criticized for dealing harshly with the first secretaries, firing them right and left. In fact, during my term in office just 60 percent of the first secretaries of provincial committees were replaced. Yet Gorbachev replaced some 66 percent of the provincial committees' first secretaries. So Comrade Gorbachev and I might well argue over which of us overdid things on the personnel question.

But the whole point was that both for him and for me there was no alternative but to replace the officials who were putting the brakes on the process of *perestroika*. They were all people hopelessly tainted with the Brezhnevite philosophy of stagnation, who perceived the power they were given as nothing but a means of achieving personal prosperity and status. They were nothing but tin-pot lords of their little fiefs. How could it have been possible to allow them to keep their jobs? If one judges by the severity with which my policy was later criticized, apparently they should all have been left in place.

The tragic case of the former first secretary of the Kiev district committee of the Moscow party was very painful for me. Six months after leaving the district committee, he was working in the Ministry of Nonferrous Metals as deputy head of the personnel department, a job that so far as anyone knew suited him perfectly well. Then, unexpectedly, after a telephone call, he committed suicide by throwing himself out of a seventh-story window. Later, when I was out of favor and was being persecuted, someone tried to use this tragic incident for his own ends, claiming that this man had committed suicide because I dismissed him from his post. A story was concocted that said he had come out of a discussion in my office and then jumped from the window. This is an absolute lie; but what amazed me most was the fact that people were even prepared to use a man's death as a trump card against me.

There is another episode from my days as first secretary that people were to remind me about long afterward. Some senior officials of the Ministry of Internal Affairs telephoned me and announced, in voices close to panic, that members of Pamyat (Memory) were assembling in the center of Moscow, complete with slogans on posters. They were holding the first unauthorized mass demonstration in Moscow for more than half a century. As many as five hundred people had gathered in October Square. They'd unfurled banners with slogans of an entirely proper kind, referring to *perestroika*, Russia, freedom, the rottenness of the apparat. One read: "We demand to see Yeltsin or Gorbachev." Valery Saikin had appeared before them several times, but the demonstrators refused to disperse. Several hours passed. The crowd began to grow. Something had to be done.

Until then only two public demonstrations had been permitted—on May 1 and November 7. Despite the Constitution, which actually guarantees the right of peaceful demonstration, there exists a tried-and-true method of dealing with this kind of event. The police are called out to surround the demonstrators and demand that they leave. If they refuse, the police start to break up the meeting, twisting arms and making arrests. The result is to bring the affair to a satisfactory end. I decided to act differently. I instructed Saikin to tell the Pamyat leaders—I believe the organization was then headed by Vasiliev—that I agreed to meet them. I gave them a choice of three places: the House of Soviets, the City Committee of the Party, or the House of Political Education. They chose the House of Soviets and went there on foot into the big hall, which can seat nearly a thousand people. When they had all sat down, I asked them to state their objectives so we could find out what they wanted. Several people got up and spoke. Some of their ideas were sound, such as the need to preserve the historic buildings and the Russian language, and objections to the distortion of Russian history. There were also some extremist remarks. When they had finished, I told them that if they were really concerned about the fate of *perestroika* and of the country in general and not about their own political ambitions, they should start by dealing with the extremists in their own ranks. I asked them to bring me their program and said that if they were prepared to act within the framework of the Constitution, they should register themselves as an officially recognized "social organization" and start working. And that, effectively, was the extent of my dealings with Pamyat. Subsequently they showed little interest in such things as the framework of the Constitution and the rules of their organization. A sizable group broke away from the organization. Though I never had anything further to do with them, my ill-wishers—to put it mildly—have accused me of being friendly with Pamyat. If the demonstrators had gotten a few blows on the head with clubs, that would have appeased my opponents.

By this time, the national leadership not only had confidence in me but also was being helpful. They realized the importance of Moscow and knew how essential it was to bring order into the administration of the capital city. To that end, the heads of the Moscow section of the Ministry of Internal Affairs and the KGB, together with their deputies, were all replaced, as were several other heads of administrative departments.

Then I demanded that the heads of the appropriate departments of the Ministry of Internal Affairs and the KGB should report to me regularly on the general situation and on any unusual occurrences. At the same time I tried to help them by mobilizing public opinion, party organizations, the soviets, and industrial enterprises to assist the law enforcement agencies in bringing order into the life of the city. We conducted regular raids throughout Moscow, putting all the police forces of the city on alert. District by district, they made the rounds of every courtyard, every cellar, every attic, and every derelict building. These raids produced good results. In addition to flushing out crime dens, alcoholics, addicts, and drug pushers, they also—to the surprise of the police, I believe—captured several criminals who were wanted nationwide. The main thing was that the raids were not just put on "for show," or as part of some one-time campaign, but were kept up permanently. We altered their timing, making sure that they were not regular or predictable, so that people who had anything to fear from the police could not adapt their movements to these purges.

Since Moscow was absolutely bursting at the seams, I wanted to see with my own eyes, and not just from statistical reports, how overloaded the transportation system was. I made a point of traveling by subway and bus, particularly at rush hours, in order to get a physical feel for how Muscovites were transported to work and back home.

I knew, for instance, that many workers of the Khrunichev factory lived out in Strogino, a newly built outer suburb. I went to Strogino at 6 A.M., and along with the crowds of still-sleepy workers I got on a bus and then changed to the subway. Then there was a change to another bus, and precisely at 7:15 A.M., the start of the working day, I reached the factory gates. This was only one episode; I made many such journeys.

En route, those tired, tense, wound-up workers told me a great deal about the way we, the leaders, had ruined the country. I resolved to change things for the better. Certain measures were instituted. For instance, the Moscow enterprises were put on a flexible system, so that the starting times of the working day were staggered. We created new bus routes and made several other innovations.

The Politburo's reaction to these trips of mine was somewhat odd. They didn't disapprove openly, but echoes of their annoyance reached me. When they began to criticize me, all their pent-up feelings came pouring out. My journeys by subway and bus, they said, were an attempt to gain cheap popularity.

This was untrue. My chief aim had been to discover what was actually happening in the transportation system and what was needed to ease the burden on ordinary people of traveling at rush hour.

As for the smear about cheap popularity, no one but myself seemed to want to earn it! If it was so easy to achieve with just a hop on a bus, why didn't all politicians do it? Somehow my detractors never felt the urge to try it, even those who had long since forgotten what popularity is. Of course, traveling everywhere in a ZIL limousine is really much more convenient. Nobody steps on your toes, nobody pushes you from behind, nobody digs you in the ribs. You travel fast and without stopping, every traffic light is green, the traffic policemen salute you—all very pleasant indeed.

I certainly didn't expect the furious reaction my journeys by public transportation elicited. In Sverdlovsk, it had been quite normal; people paid little attention to the first secretary of the provincial committee sitting in a train. If that was how he traveled, it was because it was necessary. In Moscow, this behavior aroused a storm of criticism.

During my term in office, a number of far-reaching decisions about Moscow were made by the City Committee of the Party. We accepted a Politburo directive on the long-term development of the capital. This included the very important decision to stop recruiting workers from the *limitchiki*, a practice that was having a disastrous effect on Moscow. Factory managers, given the chance of recruiting cheap labor, used the *limitchiki* to fill the most unattractive, unskilled jobs. This delayed the modernization of many factories, because it was so much easier to draw on the bottomless pool of labor from out of town than to update with new, labor-saving and efficient machinery.

123

The *limitchiki* were, essentially, the slaves of the late twentieth century under Soviet-style "developed socialism." They had practically no rights at all and were bound, like serfs, to a factory or other enterprise by their temporary work permit, by having to live in a hostel, and by the dream of acquiring a permanent residence permit for Moscow. Their employers could do anything they liked with them—break the law or disregard the health and safety regulations—simply because they knew that the wretched *limitchiki* would never protest or write letters to anyone in authority. If there was ever a hint of complaint from them, they were told, "Any more of this and we'll take away your work permit and you can go to hell." Many of these wretched people drowned their feelings of humiliation and injustice in vodka. The districts where the *limitchiki*'s hostels were concentrated were some of the worst breeding places of crime. I'm sad to report that a few months after my dismissal, the right of various enterprises to issue temporary work permits to people living outside the city limits was reinstated.

Another important effort during this period was a survey to determine which enterprises should be relocated outside Moscow. This concerned especially those factories and other plants that were polluting the city. Plans were drawn up to improve central Moscow by removing many of the countless offices and devoting the center entirely to shops, theaters, museums, restaurants, and snack bars.

Major actions were also undertaken to deal with shortcomings in the Moscow State Institute of International Relations, the Ministry of Foreign Trade, and the Ministry of Foreign Affairs. When I received the reports of the commissions of inspection set up to investigate these august institutions, I was horrified: They were riddled with nepotism and malpractice of every kind. They reflected precisely the heart of a society steeped in double standards of morality and blatant hypocrisy. In all the media, from every weapon in the arsenal of propaganda, we heard nothing but hysterical torrents of abuse denouncing the decay of capitalism, the terrible ills of Western society, and the horrors of "their" way of life. Yet at the same time the bosses of our party establishment were doing everything possible and impossible to get their beloved offspring into the schools and institutes that trained diplomats and other specialists whose jobs would take them abroad. They were prepared to tell any lies, invent any fairy tales about "developed socialism," about the final death throes of the West, just as long as they could be sent there on an official trip to enjoy a bit of capitalistic decay for a month or so, but preferably for a year. There they could buy tape recorders on their daily foreign-currency allowance, to sell in the secondhand shops on their return, making themselves a huge profit.

It was our aim to bring some order into these organizations, which for years had been immune to inspection and criticism. It was not too difficult with the Ministry of Foreign Affairs. Eduard Shevardnadze quickly sorted out the pseudo experts who had filled the country's principal department for the conduct of foreign policy. The cleanup of the Institute of International Relations and the Ministry of Foreign Trade proceeded more slowly, but there, too, it was nevertheless put into effect, through replacing the senior party and administrative officials in those organizations. Gradually the situation improved.

Tough as I am, the pace of our work had brought me to the limit of my capacity. I was working from 7 A.M. until midnight, sometimes to one or two o'clock in the morning, with Saturday a full working day. On Sundays I spent half the day driving around the fairs that I had set up, or I wrote speeches and answered letters.

Whenever I hear people say that if a boss works twenty hours out of twenty-four he is badly organized and doesn't know how to set up a sensible work schedule, I simply don't

125

take their remarks seriously. Of course I could have left the office at 8 P.M. and gone home to my family. And that would have been regarded as a sensible way of organizing my work load. But if after work I go from the office to a shop to see what is on the shelves, if I then go to a factory to talk to the workers and see how the evening shift is organized, and if I then return home at midnight, is that a badly organized work schedule? No, that is only what lazy people say in self-justification. In those days I didn't know the meaning of free time.

There were times when I would drive home, my bodyguard would open the door, and I didn't have the strength to get out of the car. I would sit for five or ten minutes gathering my senses, as my wife stood on the porch looking anxiously at me. I was so worn out, I lacked even the strength to raise my hand. I did not demand such a level of performance from others, but I still cannot stand those remarks about the boss who works long hours only because he doesn't know how to organize his time.

Despite the obvious changes for the better and the surge of optimism that was galvanizing the whole country, I felt we were beginning to run up against a brick wall, only this time around, we couldn't get away with bright new phrases about *perestroika* and renewal. We needed concrete results and some steps forward. But Gorbachev didn't want to take those steps. Most of all he was afraid of laying hands on the party's bureaucratic machine, that holy of holies of our system. In the speeches that I made at meetings with Moscow's citizens, I clearly went further. All my remarks were reported back to him, and our relationship began to deteriorate.

Gradually, at Politburo meetings, I began to sense tension in the air, which was directed not only at me but at the issues I raised. The situation got noticeably worse after several clashes in the Politburo between Ligachev and myself on the subject of perks and privileges enjoyed by party officials. I had some equally fierce arguments with him over steps that needed to be taken against drunkenness and alcoholism, when he demanded the closing of a Moscow brewery and the curtailment of all sales of spirits, even wine and beer.

His entire campaign against alcoholism was ill-conceived and ridiculous. He had taken neither the economic nor the social consequences into account. He simply plunged ahead without proper thought. I spoke about this to Gorbachev several times, but for some reason he adopted a wait-and-see attitude, although it was quite clear to me that you could never conquer drunkenness, that centuries-old evil, by going at the problem with the tactics of a cavalry charge. The attacks on me grew more bitter. Statistics from various Soviet republics were quoted at me: In the Ukraine, for example, the sales of wine and spirits had fallen by 46 percent. I suggested that we should be patient and take a second look in a few months' time. Sure enough, people were soon beginning to drink anything that was liquid and contained alcohol; they started sniffing solvents, and the number of illicit stills increased sharply.

Nobody was actually consuming less alcohol, but the income from the sale of spirits was being diverted back into the black market rather than going to the state. The number of cases of alcohol poisoning rose catastrophically; many were fatal. The situation was becoming critical, yet Ligachev was still issuing cheerful reports on the success of his campaign.

As the number two man in the party, he was issuing orders to everybody. It was quite impossible to convince him of anything; I could not reconcile myself to his obstinacy and dilettantism, but I got no support from anyone. The time had come to think seriously about what I should do next.

I still placed my hopes in Gorbachev, in the belief that he would realize the absurdity of a policy of half-measures and marking time. I thought his pragmatism and natural intuition would be enough to tell him that the time had come to tackle the bureaucracy head-on; that he could not succeed in pleasing both sides simultaneously—the party establishment and the people. You can't ride two horses at once.

So I requested an interview with him to have a serious discussion. Our talk lasted two hours and twenty minutes. Recently, when I was sorting out my papers, I found a note listing the topics that we discussed at the meeting. I had returned from it stimulated and excited, with everything fresh in my memory, and I had quickly noted it all down.

The last warning—or, as happens in the theater, the flashing lights before the curtain rises—was clear to me at a session of the Politburo at which we discussed the draft of Gorbachev's speech to be delivered on the seventieth anniversary of the October Revolution. The text had been passed out well in advance to the members and candidate members of the Politburo and the Central Committee secretaries, to allow us to study it carefully.

The discussion was fairly brief. It went around the table in order, and almost everyone felt obliged to say a few words. The assessments were positive, except for a few comments on unimportant points. But when my turn came, I firmly made about twenty separate comments, each of which was serious and substantive. My questions concerned the party and its apparat; attitudes toward the past; how the country would develop in the future, and much else besides.

Then something unexpected happened. Gorbachev, unable to restrain himself, broke off the session and stormed out of the room. For about thirty minutes the entire membership of the Politburo and the Central Committee secretaries sat there in silence, not knowing what to do. When Gorbachev reappeared, he started a tirade aimed at me personally that had nothing to do with the substance of my comments. He was letting fly all the thoughts, complaints, and resentments that had been building up inside him over recent months. His choice of words was highly critical, almost hysterical. I wanted to leave the room to avoid having to listen to so many remarks that were close to being insults.

He said that everything in Moscow was going badly; that everyone was making a fuss over me; that such and such trait of my character was intolerable; that I never did anything but offer destructive criticism, like the observations I had just been making to the Politburo; that he had labored long and hard over this draft, and that even though I knew this, I had nevertheless allowed myself the liberty of making all these negative comments. He went on talking for quite a long time.

There can be no doubt that at that moment Gorbachev simply hated me. I had known that he would react strongly to my remarks, but it came as a surprise that he should have done so in such terms, almost in gutter language, and practically without referring to the substance of anything I had said. It was small comfort to me that there were a lot of changes in the final text of his anniversary speech and that he did take into account some of my comments, though of course not all of them.

The others just sat tight, saying nothing and hoping that no one would notice them. Nobody defended me, but neither did anyone attack me. When Gorbachev had finished, I got up and said that I would, of course, take note of some of his remarks and consider whether they were justified, that those which were justified I would take to heart and apply in my work, but that I did not accept the majority of his reproaches. I did not accept them because they were biased and furthermore they had been expressed in unacceptable terms.

That was the end of the session, and everyone departed in a depressed mood, myself most of all. But that was only the beginning. The beginning of the end. At subsequent meetings of the Politburo he seemed to disregard me, although we met officially at least twice a week: at the Thursday Politburo sessions and at one or another event or conference. He even did his best to avoid shaking my hand, greeting me with a silent nod of the head and never talking to me. I knew from that moment that he had decided to get me out of his hair. I was too obviously a misfit in his otherwise obedient team.

6

March 10, 1989

Chronicle of the Election Campaign

I will never get used to it. Every time I am slandered, every time someone purposely sets out to provoke me, I am terribly disturbed and I suffer, although it is high time I learned to react calmly and dispassionately. But I can't!

Recently several people phoned to say that all the district committees of the party in Moscow had received an anonymous, methodical guide of ten typewritten pages on how to discredit candidate Yeltsin. Very soon I was brought a copy. I forced myself to read it and was once more deeply upset. Not because the electors might desert me—I assume that no

normal, decent person would take any notice of an anonymous letter of this kind. What amazed me was the poverty of
thought, the evidence that our ideological apparat could
stoop so low, could descend to such base, shameless behavior.

I never found out who wrote this pamphlet, but it must
have come from a fairly high-placed source, because it was
the obvious inspiration behind a number of immediate attempts to cause trouble for me. The district committee secretaries of the party summoned the active party members in
their local organizations to the district committee headquarters and read this libel aloud to them. I cannot resist quoting
some of the particularly memorable passages:

> Paradoxical though it may seem, he [Yeltsin], while favor-
> ing the most authoritarian methods in his handling of per-
> sonnel matters, nevertheless has no qualms about joining
> the council of "Memorial." Are not his political sympathies
> spread too wide? Besides "Memorial," whose other mem-
> bers include Solzhenitsyn, there is also Pamyat [Memory],
> with which he readily associated himself in 1987. Is this not
> flexibility of the sort that in practice amounts to a total lack
> of principle?

> He is fighting hard to be elected as a people's deputy, on
> which he has effectively staked everything.

> What motivates him? The interests of ordinary people? If
> so, why can he not defend those interests in his present
> industrial capacity? It is more likely that he is motivated by
> injured pride, ambition (which he has so far been unable
> to satisfy), and a lust for power. In that case why should
> the voters become pawns in his hands?

> One has the impression that in running for election as a
> deputy he is looking for an easy way back into a position of
> political influence.

> He is not a politician, but a kind of political *limitchik*.

132

The intention was that party officials, after reading this document, would go back to their districts and open the eyes of the workers to what a nasty, not to say repulsive, type this Yeltsin person was.

The plan failed. Of course, the party ideologues took the message to the grass roots, but what a reception they got there! In fact, many disobeyed orders and, just to be on the safe side, did not go to the rank-and-file membership. Some were simply infuriated when this scandalous pamphlet was read aloud and demanded that these dirty tricks aimed at a properly nominated candidate should cease. In the end, this brainchild of the apparat had absolutely no effect. My thanks are due to the newspaper *Moscow News*, which published an exposé of their operation. When I sat down and counted how many big and small booby traps had been set for me, with the sole aim of preventing my election, even I was amazed: The total number was enough to have torpedoed every member of the Supreme Soviet.

Saddest of all was when the Central Committee joined in. This happened at a plenum at which the Central Committee took the positively shameful step of nominating nonelective deputies from the CPSU on the grounds that the party was a social organization. At the same time, a special resolution about me was passed. The next day, all the newspapers published a decree that set up a commission, headed by the Politburo member Vadim Medvedev, to investigate the statements I had made at meetings with voters.

It began with a speech by a worker named Tikhomirov, a member of the Central Committee and one of those classic figures—an obedient and dependable pseudoactivist of the working class, cherished and favored by the system. There have been a lot of these pseudorepresentatives of the workers in recent years. In the name of the working class they chant a chorus of approval of any action by the party or the government, however mistaken, risky, or ill-conceived, starting with the invasion of Czechoslovakia, the expulsion of Solzhenitsyn, the persecution of Sakharov, and ending with noisy support for the war in Afghanistan. For such purposes, the authorities could always mobilize the required number of puppet "workers."

So Tikhomirov spoke at the plenum, declaring that the Central Committee could no longer tolerate people like Yeltsin in its otherwise solid ranks; Yeltsin was making speeches at election meetings in which he was slandering the party and even daring to make critical remarks about the Politburo; what's more, he was a bureaucrat himself, yet he continually attacked the bureaucracy in his speeches. "Once," Tikhomirov went on, "I tried to see him in his office, but he kept me, a member of the Central Committee, waiting in the anteroom for forty minutes."

That was the usual lie. He did indeed come to see me and did wait in the anteroom, but he came without warning, at a moment when I was holding a meeting with some of the senior technical staff of Gosstroi, the State Committee for Construction. But as soon as my secretary informed me that Tikhomirov was waiting to see me, I asked my visitors to take a break. I knew the man and suspected he was out to make trouble. He and I had a talk, which revealed that the pretext for his visit was utterly trivial. I wondered at the time whether he had come on his own or whether he had been put up to it. Then, when he got up to speak at the plenum, it all became clear.

I spoke immediately after him and said that his speech was pure slander. Given the situation, Gorbachev should have handled the matter with a little more finesse and disregarded this clearly frivolous attack on me. But he was evidently in a hostile mood, and it seems more than likely that this whole scene had been fixed in advance. It was Gorbachev who proposed setting up a commission of inquiry.

The news of the commission caused an explosion. I received letters and telegrams from all over the country, protesting its creation. That decision of the plenum, I am completely convinced, increased my vote at the election by several percentage points.

Tell me: Do our party leaders know that the country is short of the basic necessities: enough to eat, enough to wear, soap to wash with? Where do they live—in another world?

Since *glasnost* has been permitted, we have, it seems, been told everything. Even the political secrets of the not-so-distant past have been revealed. So why is there nothing but silence about our present rulers? Why don't we know anything about our leaders—their incomes, their standards of living? Or is that a secret?

Tell us what it felt like to live in the "establishment paradise." Is it true that the ease and plenty promised in the historical stage of communism has long been the rule "up there"?*

Gorbachev's election as general secretary at the March 1985 plenum of the Central Committee has given rise to a

* Questions from the floor at meetings during the election campaign.

large crop of rumors about that election and the origins of *perestroika*. One of these declares that the four Politburo members who supported Gorbachev's candidacy decided the fate of the country. Ligachev said this in so many words at the June 1988 party conference. In my opinion, by doing so he simply insulted Gorbachev and, indeed, everyone who took part in the election of the general secretary. There was, of course, a fight. Grishin's list of the Politburo members who would support him had been found. He had drawn it up when he was aiming to become the leader of the party. He did not include Gorbachev among his supporters; nor were many other Politburo members included.

In fact, on that occasion it was the plenum of the Central Committee that decided who was to be general secretary. Practically all the participants in that plenum, including many senior, experienced first secretaries, considered that the Grishin platform was unacceptable, that it would have meant the immediate end of both the party and the country. Within a short space of time he would have succeeded in causing the USSR's entire party organization to shrivel into nothing, just as he had done with the party structure in Moscow. This simply could not be allowed to happen. Furthermore, it was impossible to overlook the defects of Grishin's personality: his smugness, his blinkered self-assurance, his sense of his own infallibility, and his thirst for power.

A large number of first secretaries agreed that of all of the Politburo members, the man to be promoted to the post of general secretary had to be Gorbachev. He was the most energetic, the best-educated, and the most suitable from the point of view of age. We decided to put our weight behind him. We conferred with several Politburo members, including Ligachev. Our position coincided with his, because he was as afraid of Grishin as we were. Once it had become clear that this was the majority view, we decided that if any other candidate was put forward—Grishin, Romanov, or anyone else—we would oppose him *en bloc*. And defeat him.

Evidently the discussions within the Politburo itself followed along these lines. Those Politburo members who attended that session were aware of our firm intentions, and Gromyko, too, supported our point of view. It was Gromyko who spoke at the plenum and proposed Gorbachev as the Politburo's candidate. Grishin and his supporters did not dare risk making a move; they realized that their chances were slim (or rather, to be precise, zero), and therefore Gorbachev's candidacy was put forward without any complications or problems. That was in March 1985. On April 23, 1985, the famous April plenum of the Central Committee of the CPSU took place, at which Gorbachev announced the basic points of his program for the future—the program of *perestroika*.

I believe that when Gorbachev first came to power there were few people in the country who realized what a heavy burden was awaiting him. Indeed, I doubt whether he himself fully understood what a disastrous legacy he was inheriting.

What he has achieved will, of course, go down in the history of mankind. I do not like high-sounding phrases, yet everything that Gorbachev has initiated deserves such praise. He could have gone on just as Brezhnev and Chernenko did before him. I estimate that the country's natural resources and the people's patience would have outlasted his lifetime, long enough for him to have lived the well-fed and happy life of the leader of a totalitarian state. He could have draped himself with orders and medals; the people would have hymned him in verse and song, which is always enjoyable. Yet Gorbachev chose to go another way. He started by climbing a mountain whose summit is not even visible. It is somewhere up in the clouds and no one knows how the ascent will end: Will we all be swept away by an avalanche or will this Everest be conquered?

I have sometimes wondered why he ever decided to launch the process of change. Was it because he is still relatively young, and he detests the lies and hypocrisy that have almost totally destroyed our society? Was it because he sensed that there was still a chance to make one last effort to break free of the past and become a civilized country? I cannot find an answer to these questions. I would like to believe that one day he will tell us about the trials and tribulations that assailed him in April 1985.

The chief problem in his launching of *perestroika* was that he was practically alone, surrounded by the authors and impresarios of Brezhnev's "era of stagnation," who were determined to ensure the indestructibility of the old order of things. After a while, it became easier for him, and then he himself began to lag behind events. But at that all-important first moment of his reforming initiative, he operated with amazing finesse. He didn't frighten the old mafia of the party apparat, which retained its power for a long time and might easily have eaten any general secretary alive without so much as a hiccup. One after another he neatly pensioned off the members of the old Brezhnev-Chernenko team, and very soon he had gathered around him his own men, with whose help he could make any decision that was necessary.

He was to have even greater successes abroad, although the circumstances were rather more propitious for him there; after Brezhnev, any leader of the Soviet Union who could even speak normally was regarded as a hero. Even so, that was not all there was to it. Gorbachev is quite popular abroad, but whenever I see how well he is treated in foreign countries, I cannot help feeling sorry for him because he has to come back to a country torn apart by problems and contradictions. Back home, no one is going to shout at him in ecstasy, "Misha!" Life here is too stern a business for that sort of thing.

But in 1985, people had faith in Gorbachev as a politician

who was a realist, and they accepted his foreign policy based on "new thinking." Everyone realized that to go on living and working as we had done for so many years was simply impossible. It would have been national suicide. A big step had been taken in the right direction, although, of course, it was a revolution from above. Such revolutions inevitably turn against the bureaucratic apparat if it is unable to keep the popular initiative within bounds. And that apparat started to resist *perestroika*, to slow it down and fight against it, with the result that it has effectively skidded to a halt. What is more, I'm afraid it has turned out that the concept of *perestroika* was not properly thought through. To a large degree it appeared to be represented only by a selection of new, fine-sounding slogans and appeals.

When I read Gorbachev's book *Perestroika*, I thought I would find in it an answer to the question of how he sees our way forward, but somehow the book did not give me the impression of conceptual wholeness. It is not clear how he sees the overall restructuring of our house, nor from which materials he plans to rebuild it, nor which set of drawings he is using. The main trouble with Gorbachev is that he has never worked out a systematic, long-term strategy. There are only slogans. It is amazing to think that more than four years have passed since April 1985, when *perestroika* was proclaimed. Somehow this period is referred to everywhere as "the new beginning," "the initial stage," and "the first steps." Yet in actual fact, four years is a long time. In the United States it is the length of a presidential term, and in those four years a president must do as much as he can of what he promised to do, insofar as he is able. If the country has not moved forward in that time, another president is elected to replace him. Under President Reagan a number of improvements took place, and he was reelected. He turned out not to be such a simpleton as we had been led to believe—although several sore spots remained, which he was unable to cure in eight years. Nevertheless, the major improvements, especially in the American economy, were there for all to see.

With us, on the other hand, the situation has grown so critical over the past four years that today we are afraid of what tomorrow may bring. In particular, the state of the economy is catastrophic. There Gorbachev's chief weakness —his fear of taking the decisive but difficult steps that are needed—has been fully revealed.

Let us not, however, get too far ahead of my story. In 1986, I became a candidate member of the Politburo, and I was plunged into a completely new kind of life. I participated in all the sessions of the Politburo and sometimes in the secretariat of the Central Committee. The Politburo met every Thursday at eleven in the morning and would finish its sessions at varying times: at four, five, seven, or even eight in the evening.

The sessions were not at all like those that Brezhnev chaired, when the wording of various draft decrees was rubber-stamped and everything was dealt with in fifteen or twenty minutes. He would ask if there were any objections, which there never were, and then the Politburo would adjourn. Brezhnev had only one passion—hunting—and he devoted himself to it till the very end.

Under Gorbachev it was very different. The sessions usually began with the full members of the Politburo gathering in one room. The candidate members, the second category of Politburo membership, and the Central Committee secretaries, the third category, were lined up in a row in the conference room to await the appearance of the general secretary. After him the other full members would file into the room in order of seniority. Usually Gorbachev was immediately followed by Gromyko, then came Kobachev, Ryzhkov, and then the others, in alphabetical order. Like two ice hockey teams they would pass along our row, shaking hands with each one of us, sometimes saying a word or two in passing, or often simply in silence. Then we would all sit down on either side of the long table; each person's place was assigned. The chairman—Gorbachev—would take his seat at the head of the table, facing down the middle.

I was amused that during the lunch break we sat down to eat in the same separate categories. This reminded me of my days in Sverdlovsk, where I had made a point of making our lunches the occasion for an informal exchange of views on general matters: During those thirty or forty minutes, the secretaries and members of the party bureau, and sometimes section chiefs as well, usually managed to reach decisions on a whole series of questions.

Here, on the summit of Olympus, the caste system was scrupulously observed.

Gorbachev might begin a session by recalling something he had seen in the past week, including things he had noticed in Moscow. In my initial year as first secretary of the Moscow party he did not, as as rule, make such comments, but the next year he began with increasing frequency to remark about matters in the capital—this or that was wrong, this or that seemed to be going badly—thus putting me in a state of nervous tension.

The discussion of some issue would then begin—for example, the confirmation of a minister. Sometimes Gorbachev had already spoken to the would-be minister, sometimes not, in which case the candidate would be summoned to the Politburo. On his arrival he would go up to the rostrum to answer a few questions, usually of little significance, the main aim being to hear the sound of his voice rather than to learn anything about his views and attitudes. Generally, the confirmation of ministerial candidates lasted six or seven minutes.

As a rule, the discussion of any issue assumed a prior knowledge of the matters on the table for that session. Gorbachev almost never asked whether anyone had questions about the agenda.

143

In my view, we were always given the materials too late. Occasionally we were notified a week in advance, but more often only a day or two beforehand, so it was practically impossible for us to make a thorough study of matters that were of fundamental importance to the welfare of the country. We should have been given enough time to consult the experts and discuss the topic with people familiar with it. But we were never given time to do this—either deliberately or from sheer inefficiency. The questions raised by the secretariat of the Central Committee usually had to be dealt with as matters of extreme urgency, so they were discussed in great haste, largely on an emotional basis and without enough factual knowledge. This arm-twisting method was especially favored by Ligachev when he was running the Central Committee secretariat. He was not formally the second man in the party, but in fact the man in charge of the Central Committee is always regarded as such.

The secretariat meets every Tuesday. It has become a convention that the administration of the party is divided between these two bodies—the Politburo and the Central Committee secretariat. The secretariat deals with minor questions on its own, whereas if the issue is serious it is dealt with at a joint session of the Politburo and the secretariat. But despite the outward appearance of democratic procedures, matters are essentially settled through discussions within the apparat.

The apparat prepares a draft, which is approved by the Politburo, by people who are out of touch with the real-life situation and unaware of the actual state of affairs. Certain matters are discussed in the presence of senior officials, mainly those who prepared the material from which the apparat wrote its draft. Thus the process is, in fact, a closed circle. I was well aware of this, having spent six months as a section chief within the apparat of the Central Committee, which enabled me to observe its workings from within.

Opening remarks preceding any discussion were usually made at some length by Gorbachev, who sometimes quoted letters or other documents in support of his ideas. As a rule, this introduction determined the outcome of the discussion of the project or decree that had been drafted by the apparat, the result being that in reality the apparat controlled everything passed by the Politburo. More often than not, the Politburo members' contribution to the debate was a mere formality. Recently Ryzhkov has tried to break with this practice by discussing the topics in advance at the Council of Ministers or with relevant experts.

After the general secretary's remarks, comments were solicited around the table from left to right, to give all the members the chance to have their say. They usually spoke for two to five minutes, sometimes less: Yes, yes, very good . . . it will influence . . . improve . . . broaden . . . deepen *perestroika* . . . democratization . . . acceleration . . . *glasnost* . . . alternatives . . . pluralism . . . The members were beginning to get used to the new buzzwords and enjoyed repeating them.

At first, the emptiness of our sessions was not so noticeable, but the longer I participated in them, the clearer it became that what we were doing was often pointless. Gorbachev was growing more and more fond of the sound of his own voice. It was obvious that power was exerting its hold over him; he was losing touch with reality, possessed as he was by the illusion that *perestroika* was developing widely and in depth, that it would soon encompass the whole country and the broad mass of the people. In real life, however, it was not like that at all.

I cannot recall anyone at those meetings even once attempting to express a serious disagreement, though there were times when I tried to do so. At the beginning, of course, I chiefly listened, but in time, whenever I had a chance to study the drafts in advance, I began to speak out—at first quietly, then more loudly, and finally, when I saw an issue that was being decided wrongly, I started objecting quite insistently. My arguments were mainly with Ligachev and Solomentsev. Gorbachev tended to stay neutral, although if the criticism was aimed at a topic on which he had done the preparatory work, he naturally could not let it pass without comment and felt obliged to rebut the criticism.

Here it might be useful to give a few words of description of my colleagues on the Politburo, with whom I worked during my membership on the body.

I should begin with *Andrei Gromyko*, who at the time was a member of the Politburo and chairman of the Supreme Soviet of the USSR—that is, the ex officio head of state. Gromyko's role was a strange one: He appeared to exist; he did things, met people, and made speeches; yet in fact he was of no use to anyone. As chairman of the presidium of the Supreme Soviet of the USSR, he was required by protocol to preside over international gatherings and receive official guests, but because the talks were mainly conducted by Gorbachev or on occasion by both of them, he was effectively excluded from the real business of politics and was relegated —perhaps without fully realizing it himself—to the status of a purely formal figure. Gromyko was an anachronism. He did not have a very good grip on what was happening around him, in particular the events that largely form the subject matter of this and subsequent chapters. He almost always spoke at Politburo meetings, and on practically every issue. His remarks were lengthy, and when international affairs were being discussed, he felt the need to reminisce in detail about the past, about the situation in America when he had been the Soviet ambassador to the U.S.A. or about the days when he was the minister of foreign affairs. Sometimes these harmless but usually irrelevant reminiscences of an old man would last for as much as half an hour, and it was obvious from Gorbachev's expression that he could barely stand it.

This once active man was living out the end of his life in an isolated, self-created world. When he suddenly made announcements at the Politburo meetings, such as "Do you realize, comrades, that in the town of . . . there is no meat?" it would arouse great amusement. Everyone present knew that for a long time there had been no meat anywhere. Gromyko had his own, fairly elastic timetable. He would come to his office at ten and leave at six, and he did no work on Saturdays. He did not exert himself, and indeed no one expected him to. It was important that he play his part and not make a nuisance of himself. His relations with me were good. What's more, after my speech at the October 1987 plenum, while I was still a member of the Politburo, he was, I think, the only one who continued to behave toward me as before. He would greet me and ask how things were going, as though nothing had changed.

Nikolai Ryzhkov is chairman of the Council of Ministers of the USSR—in effect, prime minister—but despite his high office he has always stayed in the shadows. After the tragic events of the earthquake in Armenia, when in a situation of utter disaster he was obliged, literally with his own hands, to shake the rusty machinery of emergency aid into action, going without sleep for days on end, I believe that our people became aware for the first time that we actually had a prime minister. Even so, it is my impression that Ryzhkov finds his job difficult, especially now when the country has to be dragged out of economic chaos, out of the abyss into which it has fallen. He is a good, I would say hard-working and diligent, executive, but he is no strategist. He is precisely the kind of figure to suit Gorbachev, who has always been quick to praise his prime minister.

In my position as first deputy chairman of Gosstroi, I had to attend the sessions of the Council of Ministers. After a few meetings I realized how impossible it was for a normal, sensible person to endure such a disorganized, confused gather-

147

ing of dunderheads. One minister complains about another, who vents his spleen on a third. They stand up to speak without proper preparation and push each other away from the microphone. Naturally, in such an atmosphere, it is almost beyond the ability of man to reach any kind of collective decision. I decided not to waste any more of my time there and stopped attending. One would like to believe that the meetings of the Council of Ministers are now conducted differently. The ministers were subjected to a fairly serious purge by the Supreme Soviet, and the situation in the country is so grave that nowadays there is simply no time for such chaotic behavior and empty talk.

Mikhail Solomentsev is a Politburo member and chairman of the Committee of Party Control, which keeps a check on the personal affairs of all party officeholders. As matters worsened, he behaved with an air of uncertainty and rarely spoke. If the topic under discussion related to the decree on the anti-alcohol campaign, he invariably supported Ligachev, and they found each other to be natural allies. When Solomentsev was removed from the Politburo, Ligachev became depressed. There was no one left who would support that ludicrous decree. Fate brought me together with Solomentsev when, as chairman of the party commission, he was instructed to demand an explanation from me about my statements to the Western press. But the conversation did not proceed along quite the lines Solomentsev wanted. I refused to confess to having done anything wrong, since I regarded myself as being absolutely in the right and since none of my critical remarks about members of the Politburo or the tactics of *perestroika* violated either the Soviet Constitution or any statute of the CPSU. Throughout this encounter, Solomentsev looked nervous and lacking in confidence. At times I even felt sorry for him: He had been given a task that he was incapable of carrying out.

At first, *Viktor Chebrikov,* as chairman of the KGB, hardly ever spoke, unless the debate concerned either the jamming of foreign radio stations or the number of people who should be allowed to go abroad. He gave up his KGB chairmanship and became a secretary of the Central Committee. This sideways move on the political chessboard suited Gorbachev, and the obedient and devoted Kryuchkov was put in charge of the KGB. But, as before, all the law enforcement agencies and the KGB remained in Chebrikov's hands. Chebrikov still had the psychology of the KGB man; he saw Western subversion and spies everywhere, didn't want to let anyone go abroad, and treated everyone as a potential defector. Today's mild pluralism and *glasnost* are like a knife thrust into his heart, a blow at the system that has functioned well and obediently for so many years.

It was *Vladimir Dolgikh*'s misfortune that Viktor Grishin had included him in the list of his closest supporters; he was planning to make him a member of the Politburo and chairman of the Council of Ministers. Those who were listed on Grishin's team were virtually doomed, and indeed many of them soon lost their jobs. But Dolgikh survived. He was the most professional and efficient secretary on the Central Committee but remained only a candidate member of the Politburo until his retirement. Still very young—he was not yet fifty—when he came from Krasnoyarsk to be a secretary of the Central Committee, Dolgikh was exceptional for his systematic approach to his work and his sober judgment: He never proposed a hasty solution to any problem, although his independence of thought always remained within the bounds of the acceptable.

When my candidacy for a Central Committee secretaryship was being discussed in the Politburo (naturally without my participation), everyone actively supported the proposal, knowing that I was "Gorbachev's man." Only Dolgikh volunteered his own opinion, saying that Yeltsin was sometimes overemotional. Soon after I was elected secretary, somebody told me what Dolgikh had said. I went to see him, not to have a row but simply to hear his opinion of me firsthand. I felt it was important to learn about my mistakes and weaknesses, now that I had started to work on the Central Committee. He calmly repeated what he had said at the Politburo, adding that he regarded my appointment to the secretaryship as entirely correct but that I must learn to restrain the emotional side of my nature. Strangely enough, this episode, although somewhat unpleasant for me, did not drive us apart but, on the contrary, has brought us closer together. A particularly warm and trusting relationship developed between us—a very rare commodity within the walls of the Central Committee building. At Politburo meetings he and I would sit side by side. We would often discuss the country's problems with great frankness and criticize the cavalier way in which they were handled: always hastily, always going off half cocked. When he spoke he did not criticize but simply expressed his own view, which was always clear, concise, and judicious. He was a very useful member of the Politburo, but quite soon he was pensioned off.

Anatoly Lukyanov was for a long time the most inconspicuous among the whole of the party's upper level. He held the post of first deputy chairman of the Supreme Soviet of the USSR. When the legislature was reformed, with open elections to the Congress of People's Deputies, the importance of his role in the Supreme Soviet was sharply increased. Immediately the ingrained bureaucratic nature of this highly placed apparatchik began to manifest itself—inflexibility, incapacity for independent thinking, narrow mental horizons. Unable to handle the unforeseen situations that frequently arise in the work of the Supreme Soviet, he often gets into a panic, starts to lose his temper, almost shouts at the members, and bangs his fist. Given the present makeup of the Supreme Soviet, a first deputy chairman of this kind is barely suited for the job. With totally free electors—which I am convinced will come—it will be hard for Lukyanov to remain in his post.

General Dmitri Yazov is the classic bluff, honest soldier, both sincere and hardworking. One might entrust him with the command of a military district or an equivalent headquarters, but he completely lacks the background for the post of minister of defense. He is intellectually limited and completely unable to take criticism. Were it not for the fierce pressure Gorbachev put on the deputies, Yazov would never have been confirmed in that appointment. It is a mystery to me how anyone expects this hundred-percent product of the old military machine to effect any positive changes in the armed forces or to develop a new approach to solving the problem of national defense.

When this classic old-style Russian general contemplates the country's civilian population, he is obviously longing, in his heart of hearts, to conscript every single adult for permanent military service. I exaggerate, of course, but personally I prefer the American system, under which the secretary of defense must be a civilian. The brain of every professional soldier is more or less set in the military mold. He always sees an external threat somewhere and never quite loses that deepdown urge to do a little fighting.

Vladimir Shcherbitsky is first secretary of the Ukrainian Communist Party. This man's membership on the Politburo demonstrates to the fullest Gorbachev's indecisiveness and halfheartedness. I am almost entirely certain that by the time this book is published Shcherbitsky will have been dismissed, probably in disgrace. He is a typical representative of the Brezhnev era.

As of August 1989, however, he is still in place, albeit totally discredited. Gorbachev is afraid to touch him, just as he previously refused to grasp the nettle and solve the problem of Geida Aliev, former first secretary of the Communist Party of

Azerbaijan, when it was clear to everyone that to keep this deeply corrupt man on the Politburo was simply impossible. I supplied Gorbachev with a folder of documents and spent almost an hour trying to persuade him to dismiss Aliev. Although Gorbachev did not listen to me at the time, Aliev was finally retired with a special private pension. But why did it take so long to deal with that scandal, for which there could be only one solution?

Aleksandr Yakovlev, secretary of the Central Committee and member of the Politburo, is a most intelligent, sensible, and farseeing politician. It always gave me pleasure to hear his precise comments and analyis of topics under discussion by the Politburo. He was careful and never made a direct lunge at Ligachev, as I did, but they were undoubtedly poles apart. Yakovlev's model of socialism was diametrically opposed to Ligachev's conception of it as a mixture of barracks and collective farm. Nevertheless, they were obliged to make a truce with each other, and both echo Gorbachev in forcing themselves to utter the ritual phrases about the unity of the Politburo.

Vadim Medvedev is a secretary of the Central Committee and a member of the Politburo. After Gorbachev ordered the two chief opponents on matters of ideology, Ligachev and Yakovlev, back into their corners by giving the former agriculture and the latter foreign policy, Medvedev became the country's chief theorist. He manages the job with great difficulty, or to be more precise, he doesn't manage it at all. His chief virtues, for which Gorbachev appointed him, are obedience and a total lack of new ideas. Obviously, in today's stirring times these qualities are not enough to cope with that job. In the era of *glasnost* and *perestroika*, even to defend the status quo of the party bureaucracy and the authoritarian system of running the economy requires a more flexible and subtle mind. When I was still first secretary of the Sverdlovsk provincial party committee, Medvedev came to speak to our people, and after half an hour, without having finished his speech, he was obliged to leave the rostrum in disgrace. Even in those days, his clichés, his sententious remarks, and his stale vocabulary, which reeked of hack journalism, were unbearable. Today he deals with ideology to the best of his extremely modest ability. The main party newspaper, *Pravda*, the mouthpiece of the conservative forces, is steadily losing circulation. But Medvedev is firmly in place and will remain there until he brings about a total collapse of the party's ideology. (Recently Viktor Afanasiev has been replaced as editor of *Pravda* by Ivan Frolov, a former aide and political consultant to Gorbachev, and the newspaper's fortunes have started to recover.)

Rereading the lines above about my former Politburo colleagues has depressed me. This, after all, is the general staff of *perestroika*. These are the brains of the party, the best minds in the country.

But what did I expect? All the members of the Politburo are either career bureaucrats who have slowly climbed the ladder of the Central Committee's hierarchy, apparatchiks to the marrow of their bones, or they are former regional or provincial secretaries—such as Gorbachev and Ligachev and a certain Yeltsin, who also made their party careers during Brezhnev's "era of stagnation."

I have always understood why many decent people continued to regard me with suspicion even after I had fallen into disfavor. It is because Yeltsin is still seen as a party functionary, a former first secretary of a provincial committee. It is impossible to attain that position, still less to be promoted to the Central Committee, and remain decent, fair, courageous, and independent. To make a career in the party—and this belief is universally held by Soviet people—a person must excel at adapting his personality and convictions to whatever is required by the powers that be at any given moment. He must be dogmatic and learn to do or say one thing while thinking something else. It is no use trying to justify oneself and make excuses. The only thing a party official can do is to win people's confidence by hard work and by the way he uses his power on their behalf.

I sometimes wonder how I managed to end up among all these people. Why is it that a system perfected over the years and specifically designed to select only people of a certain type should have suddenly failed so badly as to choose Yeltsin. True, I didn't last long among them, and I bolted like an uncaged animal when I could stand it no longer, but an appointment like mine had never happened over seven decades. Something in the mechanism failed to work properly, something had broken down.

Every potential candidate for a Central Committee secretaryship or for membership in the Politburo is carefully screened. Everything about him is known: what he thinks, what he wants. There are no enigmas. Gorbachev knew about the peculiarities of my character and my independent views. No doubt when planning how to deal with the future problems of *perestroika* he must have thought it necessary to have someone in the Politburo who would not behave obediently. But then his attitude toward these things changed. He fell more and more into the grip of the processes of power, the urge to be in control, and he wanted to feel that power, constantly and permanently. He wanted only *his* orders to be carried out, only *his* opinion to be final, ultimate, and correct. He very quickly became accustomed to this, and he had no more use for anyone who was likely to argue with him.

The yes-man attitude toward Gorbachev has filtered down from the top of the pyramid of party rule to the lower levels. The way the Central Committee apparat works is unique. We often curse the ministries because they produce nothing yet are always sitting on the backs of the enterprises they control. Even so, they deserve credit for contributing, however indirectly, to any success achieved by their particular sector of the national economy. But the Central Committee really does produce absolutely nothing at all, except paper. And the success of what it does is gauged by those mountains of utterly useless information—sheets, reports, summaries, analyses, projects, and plans. Nowadays the apparat is as good—or as bad—as the Politburo and the Central Committee themselves. It does not exist to analyze the situation, to work out the party's strategy and tactics. It functions to provide an ideological service to the top leaders of the party. In the recent past, for instance, Brezhnev coined the phrase "developed socialism" as a description of the current phase in the evolution of Soviet society, whereupon the whole huge machine of the Central Committee started churning out myths about it: how well we were living under "developed socialism," how it was progressing and would progress, something about its stages and the path it was taking.

Initially Gorbachev had his own perception of *perestroika*, a more cautious version than his later view, and the Central Committee juggernaut obediently manufactured explanations for this relatively restrained conception of the country's future development. In time Gorbachev was compelled to move to the "left" under the pressure of circumstances, and the Central Committee apparat obediently announced the different but also uniquely correct path that was being mapped out by the general secretary, all of this being done on the "anything you say, sir" principle.

Then there is the tragic story of Gorbachev's announcement, during a visit to VAZ, the Volga Automobile Factory, at Tolyatti, that in the near future the USSR would manufacture the best car in the world. The press and television, as usual, picked this up and turned it into a slogan urging people on to ever greater achievements. The engineers and technicians, however, were overcome with shame and horror upon hearing about this. To make such a claim was to reveal a total lack of understanding about the country in which we live. A car is not just pieces of metal attached to an engine; it is a highly complex chain of interactions between design, engineering, and manufacture. It involves roads, service facilities, and spare parts. Remove only one link in that chain and the whole project collapses—how good your car is becomes irrelevant. But he had to say, "We will produce the best car in the world!" And the point is that it wasn't even Gorbachev who thought it up; someone prompted him. If the statement had been his own, it would have been possible to qualify or explain it in order to avoid disgrace. But no, with the aid of the party's highly efficient propaganda machine, it has always been our practice to pass off even the most rank nonsense as the pinnacle of human sagacity, ingenuity, and wisdom.

A party mechanism run by full-time salaried officials is necessary but not in such overblown proportions as at present. It needs to be drastically reduced in size. It should be staffed by the best brains in the party, in order that it may analyze any situation and determine clear paths for future development. This is particularly important when one takes into account the role that the party plays in our society. Has a single source of conflict ever been foreseen and predicted, has a single crisis ever been instantly and correctly resolved? Any such serious problem quickly reaches a stage of apparent insolubility, then an apparently ad hoc and invariably wrong solution is applied.

Think of all the words that were uttered about the story of the secret protocols to the Molotov-Ribbentrop pact spread by the bourgeois propagandists. How many times did Gorbachev have to say that it was all a pack of lies? Yet it was obvious to any sensible person that it was pointless to go on denying what everybody has long known to be true. Then, after a while, we admit that yes, the secret protocols do exist. But how much respect and credibility have we lost for behaving with such woodenheaded obstinacy?

These are just a few examples of the way the Central Committee works, issuing its orders and instructions to the country. But I repeat: The apparat as such is not at fault. It is simply that the party leadership is obsequious, obedient, and unchanging. An intelligent, independent-minded official of the Central Committee is a combination of words so paradoxical that one's tongue cannot even utter them.

Obsequiousness and obedience are rewarded in turn by privilege: special hospitals, special vacation retreats, the excellent Central Committee canteen, the equally excellent service for home delivery of groceries and other goods, the Kremlin telephone system, the free transportation. The higher you climb up the professional ladder, the more comforts surround you and the harder and more painful it is to lose them. Therefore the more obedient and dependable you become. It has all been most carefully devised: A section chief does not have a personal car, but he has the right to order one from the Central Committee car pool for himself and his immediate staff. The deputy head of a department already has his personal Volga, while the head has another and better Volga, fitted with a car phone.

But if you have climbed all the way to the top of the establishment pyramid, then it's full communism! And it turns out that there was no need of the world revolution, maximum labor productivity, and universal harmony in order to have reached that ultimate, blissful state as prophesied by Karl Marx. It is perfectly possible to attain it in one particular country—for one particular group of people.

In using the word "communism," I am not exaggerating. It is not simply a metaphor for an overbright Communist future: "From each acording to his abilities, to each according to his needs." And so it is for those at the top of the party pyramid. I have already mentioned their abilities, which, alas, are not outstanding. But their needs! Their needs are so great that so far it has only been possible to create real communism for a couple of dozen people—communism is created for them by the ninth directorate of the KGB, and this all-

157

powerful directorate can do anything. The life of a party leader is beneath its unsleeping, all-seeing eye, and it satisfies his every whim. A dacha behind a high green fence encircling spacious grounds alongside the Moscow River, with a garden, tennis courts, and playing fields, a bodyguard under every window and an alarm system. Even at my level as a candidate member of the Politburo, my domestic staff consisted of three cooks, three waitresses, a housemaid, and a gardener with his own team of assistant gardeners. Long accustomed to doing everything with our own hands, we simply didn't know what to do with ourselves. And surprisingly, all this luxury was incapable of producing either comfort or convenience. What warmth can there be in a marble-lined house?

It was almost impossible to meet anybody or do anything in the ordinary normal way. If you wanted to go to the cinema, the theater, a museum, indeed any public place, a whole squad of heavies was sent there in advance. They would check and cordon off the whole place, and only then could you go yourself. But the dacha had its own cinema, and every Friday, Saturday, and Sunday a projectionist would arrive, complete with a selection of films.

As for medical treatment, the medicines and equipment are all imported, all of them the last word in scientific research and technology. The rooms in the Kremlin hospital are huge suites, also surrounded by luxury: porcelain, crystal, carpets, and chandeliers. Afraid of taking responsibility, an individual physician never makes an independent decision, and diagnoses and treatments are invariably agreed upon by a group of five to ten doctors, sometimes including the most highly qualified specialists. Yet in Sverdlovsk I was looked after by one general practitioner, Tamara Kurushina, who knew me inside and out, always made a precise diagnosis in any situation, and prescribed the treatment herself, whether it was for a headache, a cold, or just general debility.

I regarded those faceless groups of consultants with great

158

suspicion, and since I have gone back to my usual polyclinic, my head has stopped aching and I have begun to feel much better all around. I haven't been to see a doctor for several months. It may be coincidence, but it is also symbolic. When you are a member of the Politburo, your personal physician is obliged to examine you every day, but a lack of professional and personal freedom hangs over him like a sword of Damocles.

The Kremlin ration, a special allocation of normally unobtainable products, is paid for by the top echelon at half its normal price, and it consists of the highest-quality foods. In Moscow, a total of some forty thousand people enjoy the privilege of these special rations, in various categories of quantity and quality. There are whole sections of GUM—the huge department store that faces the Kremlin across Red Square—closed to the public and specially reserved for the highest of the elite, while for officials a rung or two lower on the ladder there are other special shops. And so on down the scale, all organized by rank. All are called "special": special workshops, special dry cleaners, special polyclinics, special hospitals, special houses, special services. What a cynical use of the word! A specialist is supposed to be someone who has a particular training or talent. There was a time when a highly skilled craftsman really was a specialist. Nowadays in our country the word "special" has a specific meaning, of which we are all too well aware. It is applied to the excellent food products that are prepared in special kitchens and are subjected to special medical tests; to the medicines packed in several layers of wrapping paper and guaranteed safe by the signatures of several doctors (only medicine certified in this way can be given to the Kremlin elite). How many such special people are there, one wonders, pampered by the system even in what seem like the most insignificant details?

When the elite want to go on vacation, they can choose virtually any place in the warm south. There is bound to be a special dacha there. For the rest of the year these dachas are empty. There are other opportunities to go on leave too, because a two-week winter holiday supplements the summer break. Excellent sports facilities exist for "special" use only, for example on the Lenin Hills—indoor and outdoor tennis courts, a large swimming pool, and a sauna. Then there are the personal airplanes, an IL-62 or a TU-134 in which a Central Committee secretary, a candidate member, or a full member of the Politburo flies alone, except for his bodyguard and the cabin crew.

The joke is that none of these riches belong to those who enjoy the special privileges. All these marvelous things—dachas, rations, a stretch of seaside fenced off from everyone else—belong to the system. And just as the system has given them, so can it take them away. It is an idea of pure genius. A man—Ivanov, say, or Petrov—climbs his way up the career ladder, and the system gives him one class of special privileges. Then, as he rises higher, another class. The higher he goes, the more special are the delights handed out to him. Soon Ivanov begins to think he is an important person. He eats what ordinary mortals only dream of, takes his holidays in places where the proletariat are not even allowed to come near the surrounding fence. And stupid Ivanov doesn't realize that it is not *he* who is being thus favored by the position he occupies, and that if he suddenly stops serving the system faithfully, Petrov or somebody else will instantly be put in his place. Within this system nothing belongs to the individual. Stalin cunningly brought this machinery to such a state of perfection that even the wives of his immediate colleagues did not belong to them. They, too, belonged to the system. The system could take those wives away and imprison them, just as Stalin imprisoned the wives of Kalinin and Molotov, and neither man dared to utter so much as a squeak of protest.

Times have changed, but the essence of the system remains

the same. As before, a wide selection of perks is being handed out to the position that a person occupies, but each "gift"— from a soft armchair with its numbered metal tag on up to the bottle of normally unavailable medicine stamped "safe" by the fourth directorate of the KGB—bears the seal of the system. This is so the individual (who, as before, is no more than a little cog in the machine) will never forget to whom all this really belongs.

Here are some examples of the privilege system, based on my own experience. Every Central Committee secretary, every member or candidate member of the Politburo, is assigned an officer in charge of his bodyguard; this man is his aide-de-camp and organizes his life. My bodyguard commander, a most attentive man, was named Yuri Fyodorovich. One of his chief duties was to see to the fulfillment of any wish that might be expressed by his . . . I almost said lord and master, for whose safety and comfort he was responsible.

Do you want a new suit? Precisely at the appointed hour comes a discreet knock on the door of your office. In walks a tailor, who takes your measurements and returns the next day for a fitting. Soon you have an elegant new suit.

Do you need a present for your wife for March 9, International Women's Day in the USSR? No problem: You are brought a catalog with a choice of gifts to satisfy even the most sophisticated taste. All you have to do is choose! The attitude toward families is most considerate. There is a Volga for their use, bearing prestigious Kremlin license plates, with drivers working in shifts, taking your wife to work or the children to and from the dacha. The big ZIL, of course, is reserved for the father of the family.

Sometimes this essentially cynical system will exhibit an equally cynical lapse where the immediate family members of the head of the clan are concerned. When, for instance, the chief bodyguard was instructing my wife and children that they must not feed me fruit and vegetables bought in the market because they might be poisoned, one of my daughters asked timidly whether she and my wife might eat market-bought produce. She was told that they could but that I must not. In other words, you can go ahead and be poisoned, but he is sacred.

Muscovites usually stop and watch whenever a government ZIL flashes past, with a hiss of tires, at great speed. They do not watch out of any great respect for the occupant of the car but because it is really an impressive sight. Even before the ZIL has driven out of your gateway, the police all along your route have been notified. The lights are green all the way, the car races ahead without a stop, and you drive quickly and pleasantly. Senior party officials have forgotten that there are such things as traffic jams and red lights.

Politburo members are escorted by an additional car, a Volga. When I received a number of threatening letters, I was allotted a Volga to accompany me. Demanding that it be removed, I was told that matters concerning my personal security were outside my competence. Thus for a while it became impossible to kill me. I was surrounded by extra guards. Fortunately, they were soon reassigned.

The ZIL, however, was with me around the clock. Wherever I might be, the car and its radio were always near. If I drove out of town to spend the night at the dacha, the driver was put up in a special lodge so as to be ready to drive away at any moment. The dacha is a story in itself. As I mentioned earlier, before it was assigned to me, it had been occupied by Gorbachev, who had moved into another, specially built for him.

When I drove up to the dacha for the first time, I was met at the door by the commander of the bodyguard, who introduced me to the domestic staff. Then we began our inspection of the house. Even from the outside I had been overwhelmed by the size of the place. I entered a hall measuring about thirty by fifteen feet, with an enormous fire-place, marble paneling, parquet floor, large carpets, chandeliers, and luxurious furniture. We went on, passing through first one room, then a second, a third, and a fourth, each of which sported a television set. Also on the ground floor was an enormous veranda with a glass roof, and a small movie theater–cum–billiard room. I lost count of the number of bathrooms and lavatories. There was a dining room with an incredible thirty-foot-long table and behind it a kitchen big enough to feed an army, with a refrigerator that constituted a separate underground room. We went up the steps of a broad staircase to the second floor. Again there was a vast hallway with an open fireplace, and a door opened into the solarium, furnished with rocking chairs and chaise longues. After that came the study, the bedrooms, two more rooms, intended for I know not what, more lavatories and bath-rooms. Everywhere was crystal, antique and modern chan-deliers, oak and parquet floors.

When we finished the tour of inspection, the commander of the bodyguard, beaming with delight, asked me what I thought. I mumbled something inarticulate; my wife and daughters were too overcome and depressed to reply. We were shattered by the senselessnes of it all. I will not even bother to discuss such notions as social justice, the stratifica-tion of society, and the huge differences in standards of living; all that goes without saying. But what was the point of the whole thing? Why was it thought necessary to give expression to such an absurd degree to the fantasies of property, plea-sure, and megalomania harbored by the party elite? No one, not even the most outstanding public figures of the contem-porary world, could possibly find a use for so many rooms, lavatories, and television sets all at the same time.

And who pays for all this? The KGB. It would be interesting to know, by the way, how all this expenditure is accounted for and under what heading of the KGB's budget. Combating spies? Subversion of foreigners by bribery? Or perhaps a more romantic heading, such as satellite intelligence in space.

There is also a wide choice of places at which to spend one's holidays: Pitsunda and Gagra on the Georgian coast of the Black Sea; the Crimea; the Valdai Hills, a beautiful region midway between Moscow and Leningrad. The senior officer of one's bodyguard was given, if I'm not mistaken, about four thousand rubles—just for out-of-pocket expenses. In other words, there was no need to spend one's money on the holiday. These summer dachas are as luxurious as the year-round residences. One is driven to the beach by car, even though the distance is no more than a couple of hundred yards. I used to walk as part of my attempt to get a little exercise. I also organized two volleyball teams. My daughter and I, my assistant, and my driver played against the guards. They were young, strong, and fit, but even so we often won. In short, I tried my best to introduce something human, competitive, and energetic into that oasis of artificial Communist perfection.

It may be a somewhat controversial opinion of mine, but I do believe that *perestroika* would not have ground to a halt, despite the tactical mistakes that have been made, if only Gorbachev had been able to get rid of his reluctance to deal with the question of the leadership's privileges—if he himself had renounced all those completely useless, though pleasant, customary perquisites; if he had not built a new house for himself on the Lenin Hills and a new dacha outside Moscow; if he had not had his dacha at Pitsunda rebuilt and then an ultramodern one put up at Thorosin in the Crimea. And then, to cap it all, at the Congress of People's Deputies he announced with pathos that he has no personal dacha. Doesn't he realize how hypocritical that sounded? Everything might have happened differently had the people known all

164

this, because they would have lost faith in his slogans and appeals. Without faith even the best and most enlightened changes in our society will be impossible to accomplish. And when people know about the blatant social inequality that persists, they see that their leader is doing nothing to correct the elite's shameless appropriation of luxuries paid for from the public purse, then the last droplets of the faith will evaporate.

Why has Gorbachev been unable to change this? I believe the fault lies in his basic cast of character. He likes to live well, in comfort and luxury. In this he is helped by his wife. She, unfortunately, is unaware of how keenly and jealously millions of Soviet people follow her appearances in the media. She wants to be on view, to play a noticeable part in the life of the country. No doubt in a rich, prosperous, contented society that would be accepted as natural and normal —but not in our country, at least not at this time.

Gorbachev, too, is at fault. He is sensitive to people's reactions, but how can he respond to them when he has no direct, open contact with the people? His meetings with workers in public are nothing but a masquerade: A few people stand talking to Gorbachev, while all around them is a solid ring of bodyguards. Those chosen to play the part of "the people" have been carefully screened and selected, and are brought to the spot in special buses. And it is always a monologue. If somebody says something to him that does not fit into his picture, he doesn't hear it. He is too busy putting across what he wants to say.

And what about his wife's ZIL? What about Gorbachev's proposal to raise the salary of Politburo members? Such things cannot be kept secret; people will always find out somehow. My daughter, at her place of work, is given one small cake of soap per month, which is barely enough for her. When my wife has to spend two or three hours a day in shopping lines and still cannot buy the most elementary products to feed her family, even she, a calm, balanced woman, becomes irritated, nervous, and distressed.

Of course, our establishment cannot run away and hide. The moment will come when they will have to give up their private dachas and answer to the people for having hung on to their privileges tooth and nail. Even now some of them are starting to pay the price for their former "establishment" status. The massive defeat at the polls suffered by party and government officials who stood for election is the first warning bell for them. They are now being forced to take steps to satisfy the demands of the voters. But they make concessions reluctantly and grudgingly; they are so wedded to their privileges that every possible contrivance, including bald lies and sheer deception, is employed by them. They will, in fact, do anything to slow down the process of reform.

Ryzhkov announced recently that special rations would cease and that the grocery on Granovsky Street that dispensed them had been closed. It was indeed closed, but the Kremlin rations continued to be distributed as before, only now they were made available by telephone through the "special orders" departments of other stores. So nothing, actually, had changed. The party bigwigs and permanent officials of the soviets, ministers, academics, newspaper editors, and other higher-ups simply sent their drivers, who piled the shopping bags bulging with good things into the trunks of huge black cars and took them home to their bosses.

As I write in late 1989, I still don't know the outcome of the commission that was set up to investigate the matter of undeserved privileges. The second Congress of People's Deputies did not debate the topic either. I suspect, though, that there will be no more of this shameless practice. We will give up—I hope forever—the system of reserving minor luxuries for a bureaucratic caste and adopt the civilized method, where the only yardstick for material acquisitions will be the honestly earned ruble. I greatly hope this is so.

When people say behind my back that I refused all such privileges—dachas, special rations, special hospitals, etc.—for the sake of cheap popularity, to play up the feelings of the mob, which wants everything to be leveled and demands equal misery for all, I pay no attention and am not offended. I know who is saying these things and why they say them. But there are quite different people—my friends and allies—who have asked why, for instance, I have refused the special medical services provided by the fourth directorate of the KGB. Perhaps I had a cold. The necessary medication is simply not to be found nowadays: neither anitbiotics, nor simple painkillers, nor vitamin C tablets.

Let me tell you about a recent odd experience with privilege. In the summer of 1989, when the Congress of People's Deputies was in session, I was working on this book in bursts, sometimes at night after a session of the Congress, sometimes on Sundays. In other words, I lacked the time for regular work on it. In August, when the Congress recessed, I decided to devote all my time to the manuscript. In my study, of course, this was impossible. There were a million problems. Even at home I could not escape the ceaseless telephone calls, so I decided to rent a dacha for a few weeks in the country outside Moscow, where no one could find me. It then transpired that it was impossible to rent a dacha in August; it has to be done in early spring. We began a feverish search, not even for a dacha but for a little shack where I could lock myself away. The holiday was short, and every hour counted. It was then that I was subjected to a hail of reproaches: It serves you right, you and your sermons about social justice; you shouldn't have refused a state-owned dacha; you've got nowhere to work. You should have written your book—*then* you could have refused as many dachas as

167

you liked. At last we did find a little cottage. Its chief advantage was that it was a very long way from Moscow—nearly 125 miles. The surrounding countryside was wonderful—the birds, the forest, mushrooms galore. All the conveniences were also out of doors. Such were the splendid natural surroundings in which this book was born.

But to return to the matter of privileges. Naturally everyone wants to eat delicious, healthy food; everyone wants the doctor to be kind and attentive; and everyone would like a holiday on a lovely beach. When I refused to accept all those things, my family immediately encountered exactly the same problems that confront millions of Soviet families.

Altogether, we long to live as the rest of the civilized world lives. And that is the reason I don't understand why Gorbachev proudly announced to the Congress that he did not own a private dacha. What is there to be proud of? It is a disgrace that he doesn't own one. The general secretary ought to have a private dacha, built with his own money earned by the sweat of his brow, just like a workman, a writer, an engineer, or a teacher. But a state dacha on loan suits him better.

As long as no one can build or buy his own dacha, as long as we continue to live in such relative poverty, I refuse to eat caviar followed by sturgeon; I will not race through the streets in a car that can ignore traffic lights. I cannot swallow excellent imported medicines, knowing that my neighbor's wife can't get an aspirin for her child. Because to do so is shameful.

Writing all this evokes a host of thoughts about our country: about the direction we have chosen; about the reasons for our low standard of living; about the perpetual shortages; about spiritual values; about morality and the future.

Many people are concerned with a big question: Where are we going? Are we building the right house, the kind we need, in which we may not necessarily prosper but at least lead a decent existence? At the moment, our society is trying as hard as it can to give old ideas a thorough shaking up and to find, at last, the right way to go. So far we have strayed and gotten lost. The ways back to the high ground are blocked with lies and with every kind of dogmatic trash, and we all have to work hard in order to escape the debris of the past.

If one is to believe the textbooks, we built socialism long ago. But then for some reason we began to build annexes until we had built it fully and fully, in the words of Khrushchev. But to the theorists even this was not enough; they announced, with the help of Leonid Brezhnev, the emergence of something called "developed socialism." Now they are racking their brains over what to call the next stage. After all, they must call it something. We seem unable to manage without these labels. The Soviet way of life, if we believe our theoreticians, is characterized by no less than twenty-six specific features. Soon, no doubt, there will prove to be at least as many varieties of socialism.

In one puts the theory and the practice of socialism side by side and, with an unprejudiced eye, compares them, it becomes clear that of all its classic components, the only one to have been put into effect is the socialization of property. And even that has been done very crudely. The other elements of socialism are either completely missing from our society or have been so heavily retouched as to be unrecognizable.

To have an idea of where we are going, we need to know where we've come from. In the 1920s, Stalin successfully blocked off the democratic route and began to steer us forcibly along the road of the authoritarian state, of "socialism" administered by a vast bureaucracy. Democracy was nipped in the bud, and a voiceless, stifled population could do nothing but create a caricature of socialist society. The people, deprived of free speech, were unable to reach any agreement among themselves. Countless intimidating gestures were used against them, accompanied by a total lack of political

dialogue between the party and the people. A political dictatorship was imposed, backed by terror.

A quite different prospect was offered to us by the promised
democratization of society, in which individual interest and
individual responsibility would be paramount. To that should
be added a withdrawal of state subsidies from industry that is
genuine and not merely a cover-up for hidden subsidies. But
alas, it has not happened: Subsequent economic policy has
been devised exclusively on the basis of "public interest." Beneath this umbrella, all the most unsuitable and inefficient
methods of economic management have remained in place
and have been successfully manipulated by Soviet bureaucrats, who interpret the public interest as meaning their own
narrow, self-serving aims—which in practice have nothing to
do with the interests of the worker or the peasant.

Much is being written about the renewal of Soviet socialism; but that is, to put it mildly, a poor way of defending
socialism. It is only possible to renew something that already
exists in time and space. If a house has been built, you can
remodel it, add on to it, extend and reconstruct it. But what
if it doesn't exist at all? My view is this: We are still building
socialism. We need an intellectually honest, truly scientific
theory that would be capable of generalizing and, without
grinding any axes, assessing and drawing conclusions from
our experience of the past seventy years. We must acknowledge that dogmatic conceptions of socialism will not disappear overnight. They will continue to feed on the inertia of
the past.

The absolute insistence on the primacy of economic factors
—to the detriment of the social and political dimensions—
has affected the general strategy of *perestroika*. Economic
reforms were not complemented soon enough with simulta-
neous restructuring of political institutions. Indeed, it would
have been better if political reforms had *preceded* economic
change.

Perestroika should have begun with the party and its apparat. The party's role in society and its principal functions should have been clearly defined. Because this was not done, for a time we were trying to restructure the economy while still in thrall to dogmas and traditions inherited from a dead past and without a comprehensive package of new legislation on poverty, land, cooperatives, renting, the tax system, and price formation.

Today, by accelerating political reform, we are trying to make up for lost time. Even the little that has been done has led to a healthy and noticeable politicization of public opinion. The people have begun to take an active part in politics.

Popular power in politics, which begins with people's diplomacy, has enlarged the arsenal of its means, forms, and methods. Public opinion was literally galvanized by the miners' strikes in 1989 and the formation of strike committees. The national press has been supplemented by the publications put out by the unofficial organizations—funds, initiative groups, and others. In several republics and regions, national fronts have been formed and are in action, many of them almost thought of as new political parties. I am in favor of the creation of national fronts, but only on the condition that their programs and actions do not run counter to accepted human values. In the Baltic republics, the national fronts have raised questions that the party has always refused to face: the problems of ethnic independence.

Perestroika has stirred people up, awakened their constructive energies, and summoned them to a new creative approach to social problems. These emerging forms of popular political expression must occupy a suitable place in society. They should serve as a rallying point for everyone who is alarmed about the fate of the country. If dissidents are excluded from the struggle for *perestroika*, it will dilute and weaken the forms of popular self-expression. Dissidents should be paid thirteen months' salary for a year, otherwise our mindless unanimity will bring us to an even more hope-less state of stagnation. It is especially important to encourage unorthodox thinking when the situation is critical: At such moments every new word and fresh thought is more precious than gold. Indeed, people must not be deprived of the right to think their own thoughts.

7

March 12, 1989

Chronicle of the Election Campaign

The television debates have just ended. We are learning the methods of present-day campaigning from the civilized countries, so now we have even such a thing as televised debates between candidates. It's not easy. The camera inhibits you and tends to make you behave not quite naturally, in addition to which you are keenly aware that it is a live broadcast.

Besides all that, it was my first appearance on Moscow television since my dismissal from the post of first secretary of the Moscow City Committee of the Party. This, too, laid a weight on my shoulders. I wanted people to see that I was in good form and had been able to survive the events of the past eighteen months with dignity.

If one is to treat campaigning seriously, one must learn how to behave on television. It is a special means of contact with the electorate, which has nothing in common with the traditional ways of meeting the voters. There you face live people; you feel the breathing of the audience, the reaction to your every word and gesture. You feel all this physically, as energy is transmitted from the people to you and back from you to them. But in a television studio your audience is the cold glass eye of the camera lens, which reflects nothing but light and your own image. Somehow you must imagine, out there beyond it, the existence of real people sitting at home, drinking tea, and most likely listening with only half an ear.

But that is all theory. In reality, we arrived at the Moscow television studios in the suburb of Ostankino about half an hour before the start of the broadcast. We sat and talked to the moderator, who explained the format and told us briefly how a phone-in program worked. Each candidate was to answer several questions that would be put to him by viewers in the Moscow area. The moderator would select the questions that we were to answer.

The live broadcast began. Yuri Brakov spoke, outlining his election platform, then I was given ten minutes to do the same. And as I said, I behaved and spoke in a less natural way then usual. But even so, I managed to explain my program to the viewers.

It is, of course, not very pleasant when you are suspicious of someone, but I must say that the selection of questions surprised me. Those put to Brakov were ordinary and uncontroversial, mostly concerning the future of the ZIL factory and the car industry in general. I, on the other hand, had to fend off a succession of personal attacks. Inwardly I grew tense, but that may have been an advantage, because I started talking more emotionally and forcefully.

174

I could understand that in order to sharpen the tone of the debate the moderator could select the questions as he saw fit. Somehow, though, he managed to pass on to me questions from people who, some journalists later confirmed, didn't exist at all—or if they did exist, never actually phoned in the question. Here is one example: "Why do you always play to the gallery, Boris Nikolayevich? Even your regular visits to the doctor are reported by journalists and newsreel cameramen."—Questioner So-and-so, at such and such an address.

Indeed, that very morning I had had an appointment at our local polyclinic, having long since declined the medical services of the fourth directorate of the KGB. When I went to register at the clinic, the elderly lady who was filling out my form—age, address, place of work—almost dropped her pen when in answer to her question "Occupation?" I replied, "Minister." Then she said, "This is the first time in my life that I have registered a minister as a patient in a district polyclinic."

When I left home that morning, a camera crew had been lying in wait for me. They took shots of me going into the clinic and coming out again. And that was all. The interesting fact was that all this had taken place at eight o'clock that morning and it was a five-minute walk to the polyclinic; in other words, whoever was watching me would have had to follow my every step to have known that on this particular morning I had been filmed taking a walk to the polyclinic.

In the television debate, I replied to that question that personally I was bored to death with all the reporters, the photographers, the film and television cameramen, who never gave me any peace, but obviously the question as to why they were always hovering around me should be put to them. Perhaps the fact that they hadn't been able to photograph me for such a long time and that there had been no news of me explained their sudden flurry of interest.

But that wasn't the end. The next day, the same television

crew, aware that they had caused me unnecessary embarrassment, went to the address of the man who had asked that loaded question, found him, and discovered that he had never phoned the television station, had never asked a question to be put to me, and knew nothing at all about the polyclinic or my connection with it. Then he asked the television crew to tell Yeltsin not to worry; he was going to vote for me anyway. The crew shot the whole interview on videotape and gave me the cassette as a present.

My campaign assistants checked the addresses of several other people who had allegedly phoned in, and found invariably that the person so named either did not live at that address or had never submitted any question.

If you could live October 1987 all over again, how would you act?

Boris Nikolayevich Yeltsin! Was your speech at the October 1987 plenum a gesture of despair, or were you hoping for support from one of the members of the Politburo?"*

By September 12, 1987, I had been a candidate member of the Politburo for months, but during that time my relations with Gorbachev and other members had grown steadily worse —no doubt owing to my difficult character. At the Politburo meeting that day, the point was reached at which I clearly could not remain either as first secretary of the Moscow City Committee of the Party or as a member of the Politburo. After the meeting I went back to my office and took a clean

* Questions from the floor at meetings during the election campaign.

177

sheet of paper. I collected my thoughts and began to write a letter to Gorbachev.

12 September 1987

Dear Mikhail Sergeyevich:

My decision to write this letter has been a long and difficult one to reach. A year and nine months have passed since you and the Politburo proposed that I head the Moscow city party organization and I accepted the post. My motives for acceptance or refusal were not, of course, of any significance. I realized that it would be an incredibly hard assignment, and that much more needed to be added to my previous experience of such work, including time on the job itself.

None of that discouraged me. I sensed your support, and I came to do the job with a degree of confidence that surprised even myself. I began working with a new staff in a spirit of self-sacrifice, dedication to principle, and comradely loyalty.

The first landmarks charting our progress are in place, although in fact very little has been achieved. But without enumerating any specifics, our chief success has been that the spirit, the mood of the majority of Muscovites has changed. Naturally the circumstances in the country as a whole have had their effect on this; but strange as it may seem, my personal sense of dissatisfaction has only increased.

In the actions and remarks of certain high-level leaders, I have become aware of something that I had not noticed before. There has been a discernible change from an attitude of friendly support to one of indifference toward matters concerning Moscow and coldness toward me personally, especially in several members of the Politburo and some secretaries of the Central Committee.

Generally speaking, I have always sought to express my own point of view, even when it did not coincide with other people's opinions. As a result, an increasing number of

178

unpleasant situations have arisen—or to be more precise, my style, my frankness, and my past history reveal me as being untrained for work as a member of the Politburo.

I cannot avoid raising certain questions relating to matters of principle. Some of them, especially those concerning personnel, I have already spoken or written to you about. In addition, I would like to mention the following points.

First, there is the style of work favored by Comrade Yegor Kuzmich Ligachev. My view and that of others is that his style is inappropriate, especially now (although I do not want to belittle his positive qualities). His style of work has also affected attitudes in the secretariat of the Central Committee. Certain secretaries of "marginal" committees copy him unthinkingly, but the real point is that it is the party as a whole which suffers. Great harm will be done to the party if all this were to be said publicly. Only you personally can change this state of affairs, in the interests of the party.

The party organizers are lagging behind all the recent splendid events. For them there has been practically no *perestroika* at all, with a whole chain of consequences. The result is that we wonder why *perestroika* has become bogged down in the primary party organizations. *Perestroika* has been devised and formulated in revolutionary terms. But putting it into effect, particularly in the party, has come down to the same old approach—a lot of inflated language for public consumption, while in reality the implementation has been self-serving and bureaucratic. There has been an abundance of paper (if you spend all your time counting tomatoes, tea, or railway wagons, of course there will be no substantial change to report); endless meetings in minor issues; niggling criticisms; careful searches for negative results—all designed to reinforce the "authority" of the party.

I shall refrain from even mentioning attempts at criticism from the grass roots of the party. It is very disturbing that people are thinking in critical terms but are afraid to say so. This, it seems to me, is the most dangerous aspect of all for the party.

In my view, Yegor Kuzmich Ligachev works in a way that is altogether unsystematic and crude. His constant references to his "experience at Tomsk" [where he was first secretary] are getting to be embarrassing.

I cannot describe his behavior toward me after the June plenum of the Central Committee and his attacks on me at the Politburo meeting of September 10 as anything but systematic persecution. The result is that what he creates is not harmony but discord in the party mechanism. I do not want to say anything more about his attitude toward the events in Moscow. But it is amazing how in two years he has never once inquired into the state of affairs in the 115,000 party organizations throughout the country. The party committees are losing their independence at a time when collective farms and industrial enterprises have been given more powers of decision-making.

I have always been in favor of high standards, but I do not approve of the fear of dismissal under which many party committees and their first secretaries are forced to work. I regard it as the fault of Comrade Ligachev that in the relations between the permanent staff of the Central Committee and the local party committee there is neither the adherence to ethical standards nor the comradely atmosphere that should exist within the party—an atmosphere conducive to creative thinking, self-confidence, and dedication to the task. Therein, in my opinion, lies the source of the party's go-slow attitude to *perestroika*. The apparat must be significantly reduced in size—by 50 percent—and its structure must be decisively altered. The value of this was proved when, in my capacity as first secretary of the Moscow party organization, I cut down the apparat of the district committee by half, although this is a small-scale example.

I am personally distressed by the attitude of several of the comrades who make up the membership of the Politburo. They are intelligent, and therefore they have quickly become supporters of *perestroika*. But is their conversion to be wholly trusted? This suits them and, if you will forgive my saying so, Mikhail Sergeyevich, I believe it also suits you. I sense that they frequently feel the need to remain silent, when in fact they disagree, so that the agreement expressed by some of them is insincere.

I am an awkward person, and I know it. I realize, too, that it is difficult for you to decide what to do about me. But it is better to admit one's mistakes now. Later, given my present relations with my colleagues, the number of problems I am likely to cause you will increase and will start to hamper you in your work. And that I most sincerely do not want to happen.

I do not want it because, despite the incredible efforts you are making, the struggle to maintain political stability can lead to stagnation, to the state of affairs (or something very like it) that we reached before, under Brezhnev. And that must not happen. These are some of the reasons and motives that have led me to address my request to you. I am not doing so out of either weakness or cowardice.

I wish you to release me from the duties of first secretary of the Moscow City Committee of the CPSU and from my responsibilities as the candidate member of the Politburo of the Central Committee. Please regard this as an official statement.

I do not think it should be necessary for me to submit my request directly to a plenum of the Central Committee of the CPSU.

> Respectfully yours,
> B. Yeltsin

I sealed the letter in an envelope and wondered for the last time whether I was right in sending it. Might it not be better to wait a little? Then I sharply rejected all thoughts of leaving an escape hatch. I called my assistant and handed him the envelope. I knew that the postal service between Moscow and the general secretary's holiday dacha at Pitsunda on the Black Sea was most efficient and that Gorbachev would receive my letter within a few hours.

What would happen then? Would he call me down to see him? Or would he telephone me and ask me to stay working steadily at my job as I had worked until now? Perhaps my letter of resignation would help him realize that a critical situation had developed in the top leadership of the party and that immediate steps must be taken in order to ensure that there be a healthy, constructive atmosphere in the Politburo.

I decided not to try guessing. My bridges were burned; there was no way back. I had worked, as usual, from early morning to late at night. Inwardly, I did not admit to myself that I was nervous and suffering agonies. I pretended that nothing had happened and that everything was normal. No one, not even my family, knew anything about what I had done.

Afterward I was asked whether there had been any specific reason, any particular impulse, that had made me sit down and write that letter to Gorbachev. I have always replied that there was not. Somehow everything had accumulated gradually and imperceptibly. Yes, there had been that particular session at the Politburo at which Gorbachev's speech for the seventieth anniversary of the October Revolution was discussed and I had made twenty separate comments, which caused him to explode. At the time, this had shattered me. I was amazed that anyone could react so hysterically to criticism. Even so, that episode had certainly not been decisive.

It had all begun earlier, in my first days as a member of the Politburo. I could never rid myself of the feeling that I was an outsider—or rather, an alien—among these people; that somehow I didn't belong within the framework of a set of ideas that I found incomprehensible; that the members were accustomed to acting and thinking according to only one man's—the general secretary's—way of thinking. As we have seen, in the party's supreme decision-making body, which is supposed to function as a collective, members practically never express their own point of view if it differs from that of the chairman, or only express it on inessential matters—and that is what is called "party unity." I, on the other hand, have never concealed what I am thinking, and I was not prepared to change when I started work as a member of the Politburo. This annoyed many there, and more than once I clashed with Ligachev, Mikhail Solomentsev (chairman of the Committee of Party Control), and others. Some of them privately supported me, even sympathized with me to some degree, but never gave any outward sign of it.

A sense of protest at the Politburo's style of work had long been growing in my mind; it was far too out of keeping with the appeals and slogans calling for *perestroika* that Gorbachev had proclaimed in 1985. The general secretary does what he wants. Everyone, in my opinion, understands this perfectly well, and they all play the game and play it successfully.

But I wasn't prepared to play it, and I would express my views fairly, sharply, frankly, and directly. To be honest, my remarks had little effect, but they profoundly disturbed the placid atmosphere of the sessions. As I have written earlier, I gradually came to the firm conclusion that in order to accelerate the process of *perestroika*, a majority of the Politburo membership had to be replaced by younger, fresher faces, by energetic people who didn't think in clichés. After that it would be possible, without going back on one's convictions, to continue working actively and seriously to get things moving all along the line. Either that, or I should resign.

When Gorbachev was on leave and Ligachev chaired the Politburo, my clashes with him became frequent. It was one of my regular skirmishes with Ligachev on the issues of social justice and the abolition of privileges and perks that prompted my letter of resignation.

I heard nothing from Gorbachev until he returned from his holiday. He phoned me and said, "Let's meet later." I didn't understand what he meant by later, so I waited. A week, two weeks passed, and still there was no invitation to meet for a talk. I decided that he had changed his mind about meeting me and would take the matter of my dismissal to the plenum of the Central Committee, even though I had expressed the hope that this request could be granted without my having to refer it to a plenum. In our phone conversation, there was no mention of our meeting after the plenum. "Later"—that was all.

The date of the plenum was announced. I had started preparing myself to deliver a speech and to face what would follow it. I made no effort to organize a group of supporters from among those members of the Central Committee whose thinking and whose assessment of the state of affairs in the party and its leadership concurred with mine. The mere thought struck me then—and still strikes me—as blasphemous. I would never have undertaken the briefing of speakers, agreeing on who should say what and when—in other words, weaving a plot. No, no, and no again. Afterward many people said to me that we should have joined forces, made preparations, spoken as a united front. They felt that such a course would at least have created a stir; the leadership would have been obliged to reckon with the views of the group, even though a minority, and this would have presented them with more of a problem than could one lone individual, whom they could accuse with impunity of anything they liked.

I did not take that course. What is more, I had not told a single person that I was planning to speak at the plenum. Even the members of the Moscow City Committee of the Party who were closest to me knew nothing of my intention. I had no idea, therefore, whether anyone might support me.

184

My closest comrades in the Central Committee were unlikely to speak up either, so I had to prepare myself psychologically for the worst.

I went to the plenum without a prepared speech; I had written only seven headings on a piece of paper. Usually I take a very long time to prepare my speeches, sometimes rewriting the text ten or fifteen times in an attempt to find the most precise and telling words. But this time I had acted differently. While I was not speaking entirely impromptu—I had given very careful thought to my seven points—I did not write out my speech. Even now I find it difficult to explain why I did not. Perhaps I was not one hundred percent sure I would speak, and I was leaving a tiny crack open in case I decided to retreat, on the assumption that I might address not this plenum but the next. That thought was no doubt lurking somewhere in my subconscious.

The agenda of the meeting marking the seventieth anniversary of the October Revolution was known in advance. I was in no way embarrassed by this solemn occasion. On the contrary, I considered it a good thing that we had finally arrived at the healthy attitude that an anniversary was not only the time for long, solemn speeches with orchestrated applause, but also a useful opportunity to talk about our problems. Afterward the charge against me was that I had spoiled the otherwise upbeat mood of this festive occasion.

In his speech, Gorbachev introduced the report on the seventieth anniversary. While he was speaking, a struggle was going on inside me: Should I speak or should I not speak? It was obvious that to postpone it was pointless. I knew I must go up to the rostrum. But I was also well aware of the storm that would greet me after a few minutes, of the torrent of filth that would be poured over my head, of the many unjust accusations of treachery that I would shortly have to hear.

Gorbachev's speech was coming to an end. Ligachev, who

was in the chair, was already preparing to declare the meeting closed. Then I acted.

I had better quote the dispassionate stenographic record:

> CHAIRMAN, COMRADE LIGACHEV: Comrades, the report is thus concluded. Does anyone have any questions? Very well. There are no questions. If not, the platform wishes to consult for a moment.
> GORBACHEV: Comrade Yeltsin has a question.
> LIGACHEV: Then we will consult the floor. Do we need to throw the report open to debate?
> VOICES: No.
> LIGACHEV: No.
> GORBACHEV: Comrade Yeltsin has a statement to make.
> LIGACHEV: Comrade Boris Nikolayevich Yeltsin, candidate member of the Politburo of the Central Committee of the CPSU, first secretary of the Moscow City Committee of the CPSU, has the floor. Please, Boris Nikolayevich. . . .

And I went up to the rostrum to make the speech that was to destroy the self-congratulatory atmosphere of that anniversary plenum—and to inform the Central Committee of my wish to resign from the upper echelon of the party leadership.

I often wondered afterward whether I might have chosen a different approach; whether I really needed to have charged in as I did, guns blazing; to have caused the uproar that resulted in such a drastic change in my life. I had, after all, been aware that there was a good chance that I would not survive my imminent "civil execution." So why did I have to do it?

Now that nearly two years have passed, I can say with absolute conviction that the speech I made then was indeed necessary, that it was the logical outcome of all the events that had led up to it.

Everyone had been wallowing in such triumph and euphoria about *perestroika* that they had been unwilling to see that it had produced no concrete results except for a few changes in the direction of *glasnost* and democratization. Instead of a realistic and critical assessment of the situation as it had developed, the only reaction in the Politburo was an ever louder chorus of praise for the general secretary. My conflict with Ligachev had also reached its logical climax. In order to solve Moscow's most painful and difficult problems, I needed the help of the whole Politburo: The city is such a complex entity, where virtually every strand of the country's political, economic, and social fabric crisscrosses and intertwines with the others, that without our joint efforts the necessary moves would never be made. I had noticed that, far from their helping, there was recently an active unwillingness in the Politburo to help the city tackle the problems that had built up.

In those circumstances, how could I carry on? I could, but I would have had to become a different person, to stop speaking my mind, not notice that the country was sliding into an abyss while at the same time proclaiming loudly that the party —organized and inspired, of course, by its general secretary —was the architect of *perestroika*.

Who can have known how those hypocritical slogans infuriated me! First the bureaucratic apparat hidden behind the party's facade had ruined the country, and now that concealment was useless. Something had to be changed in that putrid system, and yet they were shouting, "Don't touch the party; it's the architect of *perestroika!*" How could we not touch it, when it had been drummed into everyone from kindergarten onward that we were supposed to thank the party for all our achievements? In any case, its role as inspirer and organizer is written into Article 6 of the Constitution of the USSR. So who was to blame for what happened? Was it the Soviet people, that new historical entity? (This concept was one of Brezhnev's contributions to Marxist-Leninist theory.) Or was it still the institution that had been "inspiring and organizing"

187

for the past seventy years? Every day and from all sides curses are hurled at the party apparatchiks—yet we are sternly reminded that the authority of the party is unshakable. We shall not allow you to touch the party with your dirty hands!

In the two years since the October 1987 plenum of the Central Committee, Soviet society has come a long way. People have grown aware of their role, not as little cogs but as human individuals. A nationwide attack on the party bureaucrats has begun, forcing them into a feverish, terrified defense of their shakier-than-ever position. But back in 1987, when I realized that I had to speak out, the climate was very different, and one was allowed to criticize only that which did not threaten the reputations and achievements of those in high places. The general secretary had become equivalent to the czar, the father of his people, and to express the slightest doubt about his actions was an unthinkable sacrilegious act. One could express only awestruck admiration for the general secretary or delight at being so fortunate as to be able to work alongside him. One was allowed to be mildly indignant at the fact that he was so modest, that he would never allow himself to be praised, and so on ad nauseam.

When I mounted the rostrum at the October 1987 plenum of the Central Committee, I had no intention that my speech would become some kind of step forward, would expand the limits of *glasnost*, or reduce the area that was beyond criticism. None of this entered my head. The important thing was to screw up my courage and say what I had to say.

Since, as I have already mentioned, I did not write out my speech but had only jotted down a few headings on a small sheet of paper, I think it would be useful to quote from the transcript that was published in the second issue for 1988 of the *Bulletin of the Central Committee of the CPSU*:

YELTSIN: The reports made today on the seventieth anniversary celebrations were discussed in draft form in the Politburo. In view of the fact that I, too, made some suggestions for insertion into the text and some of them were accepted, I therefore have no comments to make on that report today, and I fully endorse it. I would like, however, to raise a number of issues that have been causing me some concern during my time as a member of the Politburo. I entirely agree that at the present time some very great difficulties have arisen in the process of *perestroika*, and that this lays great responsibility and great obligations upon all of us. I believe that above all we need to restructure the work of the party committees, indeed of the party as a whole, beginning with the secretariat of the Central Committee, a point that was made at the June plenum of the Central Committee. I cannot help remarking that although five months have passed since then, nothing has changed in the style of work of either the secretariat of the Central Committee or of Comrade Ligachev. Despite the fact that Mikhail Sergeyevich [Gorbachev] said here today that bullying reprimands are not permissible at any level, they are still used. This form of coercion is used by party bosses in industrial enterprises and in other organizations of all kinds, but they are intolerable at any level, especially now, at a time when the party has to set out on a revolutionary course and act in a revolutionary way. There is no sign of any such revolutionary energy or party comradeliness in the Central Committee's attitude toward grass-roots party committees and many individual party members.

It seems to me that we must draw lessons from the past, that we really must fill in those blank spots in our history books and study them, as Mikhail Sergeyevich said today; and while drawing the conclusions that apply to the present, we must above all draw conclusions for tomorrow. What must we do? How are we to put right what was done and make sure the same mistakes can never be made again? Because in the past our Leninist principles have simply been discredited, and subsequently this has led to the fact that those Leninist plrinciples have been largely banished from the standards of behavior in our party.

Despite what was said at the party congress about what *perestroika* was to achieve in two or three years, two years, or nearly two years, have already passed, and now we are again told that it needs an additional two or three years. This greatly confuses people, the party and the population as a whole, since we, who are aware of the people's mood, can now sense the tidal wave of their attitudes toward *perestroika*. At first there was a tremendous surge of enthusiasm. It maintained a great intensity up to and including the January 1987 plenum of the Central Committee of the CPSU. Then, after the June plenum of the Central Committee, people's faith began to ebb, and that worries us very much indeed. This happened, of course, because those two years were largely spent in drafting all those documents, which never got to the people. They became uneasy, since they were given nothing concrete during that time.

It therefore seems to me that perhaps this time we must adopt a more cautious approach to the announcement of a realistic timetable for *perestroika* in the next two years. We understand that this is all proving very difficult to implement, and even if we start now (and it must be done) to introduce far-reaching revolutionary changes in the work of the party—specifically the party and the party committees—that cannot be done in two years. And I would say that after two years we may well find that in the eyes of the people the party's authority has drastically fallen.

I must say that the repeated request to the Central Committee to issue fewer documents—while at the same time the quantity of documents being issued constantly increases—is beginning to produce a certain attitude toward all those decrees all over the country. At the local level, there is a tendency to treat them with scant attention and to disbelieve them. They go on pouring forth, one after another. For instance, a call has gone out to cut those research centers that are not doing anything useful. To take the example of Moscow: A year ago there were 1,048 research institutes, and after enormous efforts made by the State Committee for Scientific Research, seven were closed down. Yet somehow the number remaining totaled 1,087, because during that year decrees were issued setting up new research centers in Moscow. That, of course, directly contradicted party policy and the decision of the party congress and the appeals that were made to us.

I have also been reflecting on another matter. It is not an easy one to discuss, but this is a plenum of members of the Central Committee of the Party, a most trustworthy and open-minded assembly, to which one can and must say everything that is in one's mind and in one's heart, as a Communist should.

The lessons of the past seventy years are harsh ones; there have been victories, as Mikhail Sergeyevich has reminded us, but there have been lessons to be learned too. Harsh lessons, serious defeats. These defeats have accumulated gradually, due to the fact that decision-making was not put in practice by consensus; due to the fact that cliques were formed; due to the fact that the power of the party was put into a single pair of hands; due to the fact that he—one man—was totally immune to all criticism.

Personally I am very worried that there is still not a good atmosphere in the Politburo and that recently there has been a noticeable increase in what I can only call adulation of the general secretary by certain full members of the Politburo. I consider this to be not permissible, particularly now when we are introducing properly democratic forms of relations among one other, truly comradely relationships. This tendency to adulation is absolutely unacceptable. To criticize to people's faces—yes, that is necessary— but not to develop a taste for adulation, which can become the norm again, can become a "cult of personality." We cannot permit this. It must not be allowed. I realize that this has not yet reached the point of a certain degree of falsity and distortion, which must not be permitted, but even so, the first traces of such an attitude are there, and it seems to me that it must be prevented from going any further.

And finally . . .

I am clearly out of place as a member of the Politburo. For various reasons. There is my lack of experience, as well as other factors. Perhaps it is simply the absence of support from certain quarters, especially from Comrade Ligachev, which, I would stress, has led me to believe that I must put before you the question of my release from the duties and obligations of a candidate member of the Politburo. I have already handed in my letter of resignation. As far as my position as first secretary of the Moscow City Committee of the Party is concerned, that will, of course, be decided by a plenum of the Central Committee of the Party.

Having said all that, I sat down. My heart was pounding and seemed ready to burst through my rib cage. I knew what would happen next. I would be slaughtered in an organized, methodical manner, and the job would be done almost with pleasure and enjoyment.

Even now, when so much time has passed, a rusty nail is still lodged in my heart, and I have not pulled it out. It protrudes and bleeds. I still find this feeling hard to explain. Did I really expect anything else from the mostly conservative membership of the Central Committee? Of course I didn't; I knew the impending scenario only too well. It had been prepared in advance and, as I now realize, had nothing to do with my speech.

Gorbachev would set the tone, then one accuser after another would come dashing up to the rostrum and indict me for threatening party unity, for overweening ambition, and for political intrigue. So many labels would be stuck on me, there would be enough for an entire opposition party. There would be so many Central Committee members thirsting to demonstrate their zeal to contribute to the moral destruction of a party colleague who had "strayed from the fold" that the number of speakers would have to be restricted.

And so it was. I shall again quote the stenographic transcript of the plenum:

GORBACHEV: Perhaps it might be better if I took over the chair.

LIGACHEV: Yes, please do, Mikhail Sergeyevich.

GORBACHEV: Comrade Yeltsin has, I think, made a serious speech. I didn't want to start a debate, but we must discuss what has been said.

I would like to sum up the salient points of his speech. First, Comrade Yeltsin said that we must seriously activate the functioning of the party, and that this should begin with the Central Committee, specifically with the secretariat. In this connection, certain reproofs were directed at Comrade Ligachev.

Second, the question was raised of the pace of *perestroika*. It was stated that a period of two or three years had been named as the time needed for putting *perestroika* into effect. The comment was made that this period was a mistaken choice; that this confuses people, leads to even greater confusion in society and in the party; that the situation was fraught with consequences that might ruin this policy.

Third, we are drawing lessons from the past, but apparently, from Comrade Yeltsin's point of view, not thoroughly enough, because no mechanisms have been created in the party, at the Central Committee and Politburo level, that would prevent the recurrence of serious errors.

Finally, he raised the question of continuing to work in his present capacity. Comrade Yeltsin considers that he cannot go on working as a member of the Politburo, while in his opinion the question of his further tenure of the post of first secretary of the Moscow City Committee will not be decided by the Central Committee but by the City Committee.

This seems to be something new. Perhaps he is talking about the Moscow party organization splitting off from the party. Or has Comrade Yeltsin decided to pose the question of his resignation from the Politburo while remaining first secretary of the Moscow City Committee of the Party? This sounds like a wish to fight the Central Committee. That is how I understand him, but of course I may be overstating his intention.

Unable to restrain myself, I could not help interrupting Gorbachev. With remarkable finesse, he had distorted and falsified what I had said. Now, it seemed, I was planning to lead the Moscow City Committee into a fight against the Central Committee. A political case had been set up against me; the tone and the keynote had been struck. Naturally I leaped to my feet then and there to protest, but it was too late.

GORBACHEV: Sit down, sit down, Boris Nikolayevich. You did not put your question of your resignation from the City Committee to this plenum: You said it was the business of the City Committee to decide it.

And I have, I think, covered all the points in your remarks, apart from your objection claiming that I have misunderstood you as to whether you are or are not asking the Central Committee to deal with the question of your work as first secretary of the Central Committee.

Have I summarized your speech correctly, Comrade Yeltsin?

Let us hear your opinions, comrades. The questions that have been raised are, I think, matters of principle.

This is precisely the occasion, on the seventieth anniversary of the October Revolution, to discuss such matters, and they contain lessons for me, for the Central Committee, and for Comrade Yeltsin. In fact, for us all.

This question must be cleared up.

You, the members of the Central Committee, know all

about the work of the Politburo. You can assess its policies and you, more than anyone else, know what needs to be said. I invite you to speak, but I won't insist. If any member of the Politburo wishes to have the floor, I will call on him.

Comrades, will anyone who wishes to speak please raise his hand?

From then on, the scenario was almost as I had expected. When I was mentally assessing the situation, wondering what arguments would be advanced to refute my remarks, wondering who would speak, I imagined that no really big guns would be wheeled up and that nobody whom I regarded as a friend would attack me. But when it started in earnest—when, eyes ablaze, people came up to the rostrum who had long worked beside me, who were my friends, with whom I was on excellent terms—I found it extremely hard to bear their betrayal. I feel sure that these people are now ashamed to read the invective they hurled at me. But what's said is said and cannot be unsaid.

As speech followed speech, the tone became largely demagogic. They all added up to more or less the same message: Yeltsin is an expletive, a four-letter word. Words were repeated, epithets were repeated, labels were repeated. How I endured it I don't know.

One of the first to speak was Ryabev, whose colleague I had been for so long in Sverdlovsk. Why did he have to do it? To prepare a path upward for himself, if not in his career then perhaps for a better pension. And he, too, began to douse me with a bucketful of filth. It was most unpleasant. Then came Boris Konoplyov, first secretary of Perm province; Gennady Bogomyakov from Tyumen province in Siberia—people who had been my colleagues and with whom I had, I thought, eaten a peck of salt in my time. But each one was thinking of himself, each reckoned this was an opportunity to earn a few pluses for good behavior. Of the Politburo members, I found

Nikolai Ryzhkov's and Aleksandr Yakovlev's speeches particularly unexpected and hurtful. I had no idea they were capable of saying such things. It seemed to me that Gorbachev
especially wanted these two to speak, because I had always
treated them with respect. Consequently, I would find listening to them painful.

I already knew that after this another long process would
begin, which I would have to endure, and that here, at the
plenum, I would not be dismissed from candidate membership of the Politburo. I would have to wait for the next
plenum of the Moscow City Committee, at which I would be
relieved of my post of first secretary, and then, at another
plenum of the Central Committee, I would be dismissed from
the Politburo. And so it was. At the end of the October 1987
plenum, the members voted a brief resolution criticizing my
speech as politically erroneous and proposing that the Moscow City Committee should consider the question of my re-
election. There was, of course, nothing remotely politically
erroneous in my speech, and anyone who later read the transcript was able to see that for himself.

When the publication of the *Bulletin of the Central Committee of the CPSU* that contained the transcript of the October 1987 plenum of the Central Committee was
announced, I made no effort to read the text prior to publication. I waited for my copy to be delivered to my home. I
read my speech. I was mildly surprised, having felt that my
remarks had been rougher and sharper, but evidently time
was to blame for this misconception. Since then Soviet society has moved far forward and many fierce discussions have
taken place, both at the June 1988 Nineteenth Party Conference and during the election campaign. In October 1987, my
speech was the first piece of criticism aimed at Gorbachev,
the first attempt—not over the kitchen table but in a party
forum—to discuss openly why *perestroika* was making no

196

progress. It was the first expression of the pluralism that had been declared to be so desirable.

I did not, however, read the speeches made by the other so-called orators. I could not bring myself to do so. Reading them would have been almost like experiencing all over again that terrible sense of injustice, that feeling of betrayal. No, I couldn't do it.

It was a difficult time. I took it all very badly. For a few days I kept going on willpower alone. I stood on top of Lenin's tomb as a privileged spectator of the Revolution Day parade on November 7, certain that I was standing there for the last time. But most of all I was angry that I would leave behind me more than enough urgent, pressing problems. I believed I had managed to give the Moscow party organization a thorough shake-up, but there was still a lot that I had not been able to do. I felt guilty toward the City Committee, toward the Moscow party members, and toward the Muscovites themselves. On the other hand, because the Politburo's attitude was hardly likely to change and, as a result of their spite, my proposals for improving the life of the city were running up against a brick wall, I could not allow the Muscovites to become hostages of my situation. I really had to go.

An interesting episode took place on that November 7. I was still a candidate member of the Politburo, since the Central Committee plenum that was to decide on my resignation had not yet taken place. On that day, which commemorates the October Revolution, the secretaries and first secretaries of the Communist Parties of the socialist countries gather in Moscow. They have come for a joint conference, apart from which each of them has a separate talk with Gorbachev. Without doubt they asked him questions about me, and he, of course, told them the whole story. I can only guess at what he said, but of course he regarded me as entirely to blame. So on November 7, though I was naturally in a depressed

197

mood, I was walking solemnly toward Lenin's tomb in the customary fashion, along with the entire complement of the Politburo and the Central Committee secretaries: full members of the Politburo in alphabetical order; candidate members in alphabetical order; Central Committee secretaries in alphabetical order; and Gorbachev, of course, heading the procession. The leaders of the foreign Communist Parties would greet him, as usual, with a simple handshake and nothing more. Then they would in turn shake hands with the rest of us. When I came up to Fidel Castro, he embraced me three times, in the Russian fashion, and said something in Spanish. I didn't understand it, but I could sense that it was said with comradely sympathy. I clasped his hand and thanked him. A few paces farther on, Wojciech Jaruzelski did the same thing and said to me in Russian, "Stand firm, Boris Nikolayevich!" In a low voice I thanked him, too, for his sympathy and support. All this took place under the eyes of Gorbachev and all our other party leaders.

This, I think, only increased their suspicion of me. They avoided talking to me, lest anyone should see them engaged in this strange activity at that point, although I think that a few Politburo members, in their heart of hearts, supported me—perhaps not totally, but at least they were sympathetic. Some of them had sent greeting cards with good wishes for the November 7 holiday. Gorbachev did not, but then I didn't send one to him either. I sent them only to those who had sent one to me. There were, and still are, people in the Politburo who understood my position, who to some degree appreciated the independence of my judgment and inwardly supported my proposals, but they were few.

On occasions such as this one, I was usually attached to one of the general secretaries or first secretaries of a foreign Communist Party, generally Fidel Castro. He and I always got on well together. But this time I was left on my own.

Naturally I felt extremely uncomfortable at the reception after the parade, and I tried to stay on the sidelines.

On November 9, I was taken to the hospital with a severe headache and chest pains. I had suffered a physical breakdown. I was pumped full of medicines, mostly tranquilizers, which relaxed my nerves and muscles. The doctors forbade me to get out of bed and kept giving me drips and injections. It was particularly bad at night between 3 and 5 A.M. I could scarcely bear the appalling pain of my headaches. My wife wanted to come and see me, but they would not let her, saying I was too sick to be disturbed.

Suddenly, on the morning of November 11, the telephone rang on my special Kremlin line, plugged into telephone exchange number 1. It was Gorbachev, and he spoke as if he were calling me not in the hospital but at my dacha. In a calm voice he said: "You must come and see me for a short while, Boris Nikolayevich. After that, perhaps we will go and attend the plenum of the Moscow City Committee together." I said I couldn't come because I was in bed and the doctors wouldn't let me get up. "Don't worry," he said cheerfully. "The doctors will help you to get up."

I shall never be able to understand that. In all my life I have never heard of anyone, whether a worker or a manager, being dragged out of a hospital bed to be dismissed. It is simply unheard-of. My complaint is not that it is a crass violation of our labor laws, because the provisions of the labor code have never, it seems, applied to politicians. However much Gorbachev may have disliked me, to act like that was inhuman and immoral. I simply hadn't expected it of him. Why was he in such a hurry? I wondered. Was he afraid I might change my mind? Or did he reckon that with me in this condition he could make short work of me at the plenum of the Moscow City Committee? Perhaps he actually wanted to finish me off physically. I could not understand such cruelty.

199

I began to pull myself together. The obedient doctors, who only a few hours earlier had forbidden me to get up and move about, let alone go outside, started to pump me full of sedatives. My head was spinning, my legs were crumpling under me. I could hardly speak because my tongue wouldn't obey. When my wife saw me she begged, implored, demanded that I not go. Scarcely able to shuffle my feet, I was almost like a robot. I understood practically nothing of what was happening around me, and in that state I got into a car and was driven to the offices of the Central Committee.

Worn out by the strain and worry caused by my illness, my wife could not restrain herself and had some extremely sharp words with Plekhanov, the head of the ninth directorate of the KGB. She told him that to discharge such a sick man was sadism; that whereas the KGB was supposed to be guarding me and taking care of me, they now might easily cause my death. And all because they were too cowardly to stand up for me on grounds of simple humanity. He, of course, had nothing to say. He was just another little cog in the system, which always functioned "wonderfully," whatever the circumstances. If it was their job to guard Yeltsin, they would guard him. If orders came to fetch him when he was an invalid, they would fetch him. I believe that if they had been ordered to, they would have hauled me, dead, out of my grave and delivered me to a plenum or anywhere else.

I was thus barely conscious when I appeared at the Politburo. I was in the same condition when I arrived at the plenum of the City Committee. All its members were seated when the entire top brass of the party entered the hall and took their seats on the presidium, like a row of waxwork dummies, while the full complement of this plenary meeting stared back at them, as frightened and mesmerized as a rabbit looking at a boa constrictor.

What do you call it when a person is murdered with words? Because what followed was like a real murder. After all, I could have been dismissed in a sentence or two, then and there, at the plenum. But no; they had to enjoy the whole process of public betrayal, when comrades who had been working alongside me for two years, without the slightest sign of discord in our relations, suddenly began to say things that to this day my mind refuses to absorb. If I hadn't been so heavily doped, of course, I would have fought back. I would have refuted the lies and shown up the treachery—yes, the treachery—of everyone who spoke. I blame the doctors for allowing me to be dragged there at all and stuffing me so full of drugs that I could hardly take anything in. Although perhaps I should be grateful to them for that; the fact that my perceptions were so blunted may have saved me from a fatal heart attack.

Afterward I would often go back in my mind to that November plenum, in an attempt to understand what made those people go up to the rostrum, how they salved their consciences and flung themselves on me at the bidding of the chief huntsman: Tally ho! Yes, they were a pack of hounds. A pack ready to tear me to pieces. I cannot describe it any other way.

Their speeches contained little real argument, consisting mostly of either demagogy, conjecture, fantasy, or plain lies. Some attacked me simply out of fear: We've been told to savage him, so we'll do it; there's no getting out of it. Others suddenly revealed a really nasty streak in their nature: At last I can even the score—you were my boss and I couldn't say a word against you, but now . . . All of this taken together added up to something terrible, something inhuman.

So I was dismissed, ostensibly at my own request, but it was done with such a ranting, roaring, and screaming that it has left a rotten taste in my mouth to this day. The entire proceedings of that plenum were published in *Moscow Pravda*. One of the first things I had done as first secretary of the City Committee was to demand that this newspaper start publishing reports of plenary meetings in full: the reports and the speeches without cuts. To this day the Central Committee has been unwilling to sanction this, because it is afraid to. Thus I was the victim of my own effort. I'm joking, of course; truth and frankness can never do harm. To unprejudiced people, that publication in *Moscow Pravda* was a severe blow. It plainly revealed the attitudes of fear, cowardice, and subservience that prevailed in the upper echelons of the party.

Then I went back into the hospital. I managed to haul myself back out before the February 1988 plenum. The plenum passed calmly enough, and Gorbachev moved that I be dismissed from candidate membership in the Politburo.

He also cautiously floated the proposal that I might retire on a pension, and my team of doctors advised me to think about it. After talking to my wife, I told them to wait, that I would consider it after my discharge from the hospital. When I gave it serious thought, I decided that a pension was not for me. It meant certain death, as I would be incapable of retiring to my dacha to grow dill and radishes. I would go stark, raving mad or die of boredom. I needed to be among people, I needed to work; otherwise I would be lost. I told the doctors that I would not take retirement.

After a little while Gorbachev again telephoned me in the hospital and offered me the ministerial post of first deputy chairman of Gosstroi. As I have already explained, at that moment I didn't care what job I did. I accepted it without a moment's reflection.

People have often asked me—and later I asked myself the same question—why didn't Gorbachev decide to get me out of the way once and for all? The removal of political opponents has always been successfully managed in the Soviet Union. I could easily have been pensioned off or sent as ambassador to some faraway country. Yet Gorbachev let me stay in Moscow, gave me a relatively high-placed job, and, in effect, kept a determined opponent close by him.

It is my belief that if Gorbachev didn't have a Yeltsin he would have had to invent one. Despite the dislike of me that he has shown recently, he realizes that he needs someone like me—prickly, sharp-tongued, the scourge of the overbureaucratized party apparat—and for this reason he keeps me near at hand. In this real-life production, the parts have been appropriately cast, as in a well-directed play. There is the conservative Ligachev, who plays the villain; there is Yeltsin, the bully boy, the madcap radical; and the wise, omniscient hero is Gorbachev himself. That, evidently, is how he sees it.

I also think that he decided not to pension me off and not to send me as an ambassador to Upper Volta because he was afraid of the power of public opinion. When I was dismissed, the Central Committee, *Pravda*, and indeed all the national newspapers and journals were flooded with letters protesting the decisions of the Central Committee and the City Committee. Certainly he had to take account of that.

I now had to lift myself out of the personal crisis I was in. I looked inside, and there was no one there. A kind of void, a vacuum, had been created—a human vacuum. Life is strange. I had always worked in contact with people. I like company; I have always been drawn to people, and I shun solitude. And when they betray you, one after another, then by the dozens—people with whom you have worked, people you have trusted—you begin to feel a strange sense of doom. Is this, perhaps, a characteristic of the modern age? Perhaps people in Soviet society have grown so hardened, after many black decades, that all the goodness has been driven out of them. It was as though a circle had been traced around me, which no one could enter for fear of contamination. I was a kind of leper, especially to those who trembled for their careers; for those who strove to please the mighty; for opportunists; and also, sad though it may be, for people who were quite normal but were also dogged by fear.

Yes, many turned away from me. The majority of them

were time-servers who had once seemed to be friends and comrades but in reality were simply there for the ride, as long as it was taking them in the right direction, for whom I was useful as a boss, as first secretary, and that's all.

At plenary sessions of the Central Committee and other gatherings, when there was no avoiding me, our leaders would acknowledge me, nervously and cautiously, with a nod of the head, making it clear that although I was, of course, alive, I was only nominally alive. Politically I didn't exist. Politically I was a corpse.

Another thing that left me vaguely depressed was the absence of telephone calls from people who had once constantly phoned. I often wondered how I would behave in their place. At least I am absolutely certain that I would not abandon someone in trouble. It would be too glaring a violation of elementary human principles.

It is hard to describe the state I was in. A real battle had started up within myself. I would analyze every step I had taken, every word I'd spoken. I would analyze my principles, my view of the past, the present, the future. I would analyze my personal relationships with people and even with my family. I was engaged in a constant, obsessive process of analysis, day and night, night and day. I would sleep for three or four hours, and then the thoughts would come creeping back.

In cases like this, people often seek solace in God; others seek it in a bottle. Neither of these escape routes interested me. All that was left was my faith in people, but it was limited now: only my true, devoted friends. None of my previous, often naive faith remained.

Mentally I summoned up the images of hundreds of people —friends, comrades, neighbors, and colleagues. I reviewed my relationships with my wife, children, and grandchildren. I reviewed and examined my beliefs. All that was left where my heart had been was a burned-out cinder. Everything around me was burned out, everything within me was burned out.

It was a time of fierce struggle with myself. I knew that if I lost that fight, my whole life was lost. The tension within me was extreme, and for that reason my strength was at a very low ebb. I was tormented by headaches almost every night. The emergency medical service would come often. I would be given an injection and for a time the pain would go away, only to return. My family supported me in every way they could. For night after sleepless night my wife, Naya, my daughters, Lena and Tanya, would sit beside my bed and do all they could to help. Especially at the onset of those appalling headache attacks, I felt like crawling up the wall and could hardly restrain myself from crying out loud. It was like the tortures of hell. I used to think my patience had simply snapped and my head was about to split open.

I had faith in a few doctors, in Yuri Kuznetsev, Anatoly Grigoriev, and one or two others, who told me that it would all pass, that it was the effect of acute strain, which only time could cure. Yet my brain never switched itself off. It was running at top speed almost around the clock, day in and day out. My nerves would give way. My moods were inconsistent, and sometimes I vented my feelings on my family. When I calmed down again, I felt ashamed and embarrassed in front of the people who were closest to me. My family had to put up with a lot during that time, but they always forgave me.

My wife and daughters would try to calm and distract me, but I was aware of the efforts they were making, and it only wound me up even more. I gave them a very hard time. And it is largely thanks to them that I managed to survive and pull out of that time of trial.

Later I heard people say that I had been contemplating suicide. I don't know where those rumors came from. The state I was in was such that it might drive someone to that simple way out. But I am not like that; my character will not allow me to give in. No, I would never have taken that step.

Although I was living the life of an outcast, I was not quite on a desert island. I was on a peninsula, and my peninsula was joined to the mainland by a narrow path. It was a human path, a path of faithful, devoted friends, many from Moscow, many from Sverdlovsk, indeed from all over the country. They were quite undisturbed that the authorities suspected them of being in contact with me.

I started going for walks around the streets. In the days when I was working, I had completely forgotten what it was like simply to go out and take a walk without bodyguards or aides, like any ordinary Muscovite. It was a wonderful feeling, perhaps the only pleasure I experienced in the whole of that black time. Complete strangers would come up to me on the street, in shops, in the cinema, with a smile of greeting. This made things easier to bear, and at the same time it made me think. Here were ordinary passersby whose behavior was more decent and honorable than that of many who had once called themselves my friends.

The fact that I was a political outcast was made clear to me everywhere, and even though as first deputy chairman of Gasstroi I was holding a position of ministerial rank, constant attempts were made to represent me as a flawed person who was very much in eclipse. In this atmosphere it was, of course, extremely difficult, often impossible, to solve problems and get things done in my new job. Those eighteen months were, in fact, a nightmare, and to be honest, I did not like the work either. Although I had, as usual, dived into it headfirst, I still felt an urge to be back in political life, for the job didn't allow me enough contact with people.

The Western press continued to take an interest in me, and the sequel to any interview I gave was invariably a scolding from the party, because I always tried to tell the truth. When

I met Western journalists, I had no wish to hide anything or to suppress any facts. For decades it had been drummed into us that the Western press always lied or deceived people, and did nothing but write slanderous filth about us. In reality, the correspondents of the Western press are more often than not distinguished by their competence, professionalism, and strict observance of journalist ethics. I'm not talking about the yellow press; unfortunately, I have had occasion to encounter that too.

I took quite a philosophical attitude toward the fact that the Soviet press ignored me. I knew that the journalists themselves were not responsible. Indeed, I saw how Soviet newspapermen would try to slip stories about me past their bosses, reports in which there was a brief paragraph or even just a mention of my name. But such stories were always censored, and more than once the journalists got into serious disputes on this score. But some articles that were unfair and malicious were published.

My relations with the intellectuals were not easy either. Someone started circulating the myth, no doubt linked to the defects in my character, that I was a leader of the Stalinist type—which was, of course, absolutely untrue, if only because with every instinct, with my whole being, I detested what had happened during the Stalin years. I remember only too well when my father was taken away in the middle of the night, even though I was only six years old at the time.

Yet it was intellectuals who refused to be manipulated by the apparat and extended the hand of sympathy to me. Irina Arkhipova, Yekaterina Shevelyova, Kyrill Lavrov, and Mark Zakharov, together with many other writers and artists, sent me greetings on national holidays, wrote to me, came to talk to me, and invited me to the theater and to concerts. I recall in particular a telegram, as funny and kindhearted as anything, sent to me by Eduard Uspensky, the children's writer

207

(who created the television cartoon characters of Cheburashka and Gena the Crocodile). I greatly cherished all these messages.

Gradually and with great difficulty I overcame my inner turmoil. Month by month I would feel a little better, though not all at once. The process was taking place. I stopped being tormented by headaches, although I was sleeping as badly as ever.

The people who remained faithful through thick and thin, who suffered for me truly and sincerely, who would come to offer me their support at the worst moments, were the friends of my student days. I am eternally grateful to them. And they still feel sympathy for me, because it has so happened that I still seem to be engaged in a perpetual conflict of one kind or another.

Slowly, bit by bit, I began to settle down. I became actively involved in the work of Gosstroi. To my own surprise, I discovered that I had not lost my professional standards as a civil engineer and that all the problems that came to my desk were familiar to me. I had feared that I might have become out-of-date.

I neither met with nor talked to Gorbachev. We bumped into each other only once, during a recess at a plenum of the Central Committee. He was walking up the aisle of the auditorium, and I was standing on one side of it, so that he couldn't have gone past without noticing me. He stopped, turned toward me, took a pace forward, and said, "Hello, Boris Nikolayevich." I decided to adopt his tone and replied, "Hello, Mikhail Sergeyevich." The rest of the conversation was connected to something that had happened a few days before.

Despite the fact that I was in disfavor and was, in effect, a political exile, I had been invited to the Higher Komsomol School for a meeting with students there. They had great difficulty in arranging this. Yuri Raptanov, secretary of the school's Komsomol committee, had taken the initiative, and he had been supported by nearly all the students, most of whom were mature, intelligent, and energetic.

Raptanov first went to the rector of the school, who dismissed the idea of inviting Yeltsin. But Yuri was insistent and approached the party committee, whose secretary was cast in a different mold, being more open-minded and progressive. He proposed that the question should be discussed at the party committee's next meeting. There it was decided to invite Yeltsin. When the rector saw that everyone was voting in favor of this proposal and realized that if he was to be the only one voting against it he would find his job extremely difficult in the future, he, too, voted in favor. The students telephoned me, and we agreed on a date and time for our meeting. Naturally everyone got to hear about this—in particular, the central committee of Komsomol—and I was told that Viktor Mironenko, the first secretary of the Komsomol Central Committee, went twice to the school to try and prevent the meeting from taking place. But the students ignored him.

I knew in advance that the occasion would be fraught with risk, and I was right. I began by making a speech, taking a general look at various political, economic, and social problems and describing the processes that were taking place within the party. My remarks immediately set the tone for keen and searching questions that were put to me, and for my answers to them. It has always been my principle to answer the most awkward questions first. Those handed up were rough and complicated to answer, sometimes offensive and difficult. There were also questions of a personal nature, as well as some about Gorbachev and other Politburo members and secretaries of the Central Committee. I answered them all. I even answered questions about Gorbachev's failings, which at the time was almost unthinkable. The meeting lasted about five hours, and I remained standing at the rostrum for the whole of that time. The audience's reaction was boisterous, extracts from the speeches were published in the school newspaper—in condensed form, but in terms that went well beyond the level of *glasnost* that was current in the Soviet media at that time. Naturally the KGB tape-recorded the entire five hours.

So it was that during the recess at the Central Committee plenum, when Gorbachev and I exchanged greetings, he asked me how I had found my meeting with the Komsomols, to which I replied that it had been very lively and interesting. He remarked that he had heard I had criticized the Politburo, saying that it gave inadequate attention to the Komsomol. I said, "What you were told wasn't quite correct. I didn't say inadequate attention; I said you were treating the Komsomol badly."

He stood there for a moment, evidently at a loss for an answer. We walked a few paces side by side. I said that he and I should meet, as problems were arising that ought to be cleared up. He replied: "Yes, I expect we should." With that, our conversation ended, as I felt that the initiative should come from him.

That was our only encounter in eighteen months; apart from it, we neither met nor spoke to each other. Even so, I had the feeling that the ice was breaking up. My incarceration was coming to an end. New times were on the way—unpredictable and unfamiliar—in which I had to find a place for myself.

8

March 26, 1989

Chronicle of the Election Campaign

Sunday. The last day. Everyone at home was in a state of mild anxiety, expressed in a slightly higher level of domestic bustle and fuss, and this was transmitted to me, although of course only my wife and children were able to detect my unusual state of mind. At one point I looked out the window and saw with horror that Western television crews were already waiting in the courtyard, right outside our front door. For several months the presence of foreign journalists had become almost as familiar to me as the presence of my campaign helpers. Lately I had been unable to step outdoors

211

alone, and it was impossible to hide from them. Of course I understood that they were only doing their job, but I must confess that it had been difficult to withstand such constant pressure.

I realized that today would witness the peak of journalistic interest in me. For the first time my wife and children would see it too—would feel what it has been like—and it occurred to me that it would distress them.

We got dressed in our best clothes—Election Day is, after all, a national holiday—and went out the front door. Immediately a horde of journalists flung themselves at us. There were practically none from the Soviet media; the crowd was largely made up of Western correspondents. They wanted to film the family's progress from our home to the Palace of Pioneers in the Frunze district, where the polling place was located. I couldn't honestly see why they wanted these "historic" shots, but they hovered all around us all the way, filming us now from behind, now from in front.

At the polling place itself the scene was quite appalling. About a hundred people with cameras, flashbulbs, and tape recorders surrounded me, pressing in, asking questions, interrupting and shouting in every language under the sun. As I forced my way through the crowd, I looked around to see how the members of my family were faring. They were holding their own, but clearly with great effort. Surrounded by this mass of people, I went up to the second floor, and there my name was checked against the electoral register and I was handed a ballot.

As I approached the ballot box, dozens of lenses were trained on me. Suddenly I was overcome by a sense of the ridiculous. I recalled the thousands of similar photographs taken in the recent past, when our aging leader had stood frozen in a solemn pose at the ballot box. He had obviously enjoyed the event, knowing that next day his photograph would be on the front page of every newspaper and magazine:

212

Comrade Leonid Ilyich Brezhnev, General Secretary of the
CC of the CPSU and Chairman of the Presidium of the Supreme Soviet of the USSR, at the polling booth.

So when all those film, television, and camera lenses were
aimed at me, I couldn't help feeling how stupid it must look
to an onlooker. Muttering "This doesn't make any sense. It's
like a flashback to the Brezhnev era," I quickly deposited my
ballot in the slot and made a dash for the exit. I don't think
anyone actually managed to photograph me at the solemn
moment when I dropped my ballot into the box. All the journalists then flung themselves after me, managing to destroy
one of the voting booths in the stampede. I felt truly sorry for
the members of the electoral commission working at the polling place, who had been overwhelmed by this tornado, and I
tried to get out onto the street as quickly as possible in order
to draw this surging mass of journalists out of the building.

For about half an hour I could not force my way out of the
solid encircling ring, while I answered questions about the
election, about my own chances of being elected, about the
past, and so on. Finally I struggled free and together with my
family almost ran from the pursuing journalists to the home
of my elder daughter, who lived closer to the polling place.
Taking refuge there, we were able to get our breath back in
peace and reflect on the events of that day. For the day was a
decisive one; it would decide the outcome of my election
battle—not against my opponent but against the party apparat.

My campaign workers were stationed at practically every
polling place in the capital. Their first job was to watch carefully for any dirty tricks or rigging of the electoral process
(although I didn't believe that anyone would stoop to that),
and second, they were to pass on to me the results of the
voting when the intial returns came in.

We had every reason to worry about the figures, about
every single vote. We had heard of an unexpected decision

213

made by the authorities, according to which all the Soviet officials working abroad in twenty-nine different countries were to be registered as voters in the Moscow number 1 constituency. Without doubt this was one final attempt to influence the result of the election. Everyone realized that our figures for these overseas votes would be dismal. It was most likely that in every Soviet embassy the officials and employees would vote obediently in line with the ambassador's preference. They were, after all, abroad. Precisely for that reason, the number of votes in Moscow had to be overwhelmingly in my favor, to counteract any votes from citizens abroad.

When the journalists on watch outside my daughter's door dispersed, realizing that it was pointless to wait for me any longer, we emerged from our refuge and decided to take a walk around the city. There was something joyous about that walk around Moscow. Passersby greeted us, smiled, and wished me good luck.

That evening I was told the preliminary results. I was far ahead in every polling district. Now practically nothing could prevent me from winning the seat.

Boris Nikolayevich! People all over the country have a very good opinion of you. Even so, it is strange that you were chosen as a delegate to the June 1988 party conference from Karelia, of all places. Why didn't you go as a delegate from Moscow? Or from Sverdlovsk?

Tell us why Gorbachev didn't support you at the party conference.

Do you remember Chikiryov, and whom he was defending when he pounded his chest?

Don't you regret criticizing Gorbachev's "cult of personality" at the seventieth anniversary of the October Revolution, instead of at the Nineteenth Party Conference? Didn't your sense of political timing let you down on that occasion?*

* Questions from the floor during the meetings election campaign.

215

Everyone in the leadership and the apparat earnestly prepared themselves for the Nineteenth All-Union Party Conference. The party, and indeed society as a whole, were expecting a lot to come of it. It is now possible to say that the conference did give a push to the development of Soviet society; it did not, however, become the historic national turning point that a party conference should be. Certain of its decisions were more conservative than the mood of the country at the time. The proposal, for instance, to combine the functions of party and Soviet leaders, starting with the general secretary and ending with the secretaries of local party committees, struck people as a bolt from the blue. Even Stalin did not allow himself to combine those two duties. The population at large did not support this proposal, but a majority of conference delegates obediently voted for the resolution.

The delegates to the conference were chosen more carefully than usual, and they were elected according to special instructions drawn up by the Central Committee. An active role in organizing these pseudo elections was played by Razumov, the first deputy chief of the organization branch of the Central Committee. Virtually all delegate matters were in his hands, and consequently the results fully reflected his sympathies, antipathies, and favoritism.

At the time, I was in exile, so to speak, working in the State Committee for Construction, and the party leadership did not want me to return to political life. But I felt the desire and the strength to start another political career from scratch. My principles wouldn't allow me to leave the political arena meekly and without putting up a fight. My speech at the November 1987 plenum was still not publicly known, and an aura of mystery shrouded that whole episode.

Party organizers around the country were starting to propose me as a delegate to the party conference, so it became a primary objective of the apparat to prevent my election. I held ministerial rank, and there seemed no doubt that ministers would be elected to the conference. I noticed, however, that while ministers were being elected to delegations from various regions, I was not among them. Total silence. There was a real chance of my not being elected to attend the conference at all. At first, I somehow didn't realize how big that chance was. But the apparat was hard at work, time was passing, and it soon became clear that I was the only minister who had not been elected as a delegate. I then realized the seriousness of the situation.

I felt that I had to attend the party conference and speak there. But I had no idea what I would do if the party apparat, which was manipulating the delegate elections like a skilled conjuror, succeeded in isolating me. I could hardly pick up the telephone and make demands to Gorbachev or to any other Politburo member, reminding him that I was a member of the Central Committee and was not being put forward as a delegate, and that this was improper and dishonest.

The Nineteenth Party Conference would give me the opportunity to explain what had happened at the October plenum, and it might also be my last chance to drag myself out of political exile and once again take an active role in public life. I was convinced—and still am convinced—that I committed no political errors in my speech to the October 1987 plenum of the Central Committee. And for that reason I felt sure that my speaking to the conference delegates, to party members throughout the country, and to ordinary people would cause everything to fall into place. It would be a crushing blow not to be elected as a delegate. No doubt that was why I did not even try to guess what I might do if the conference took place without me. Would I leave Moscow? Would I watch the conference on television? Would I ask

Razumov for a ticket to the visitor's gallery? No, I could not contemplate the idea, even hypothetically. I had to become a delegate; no alternative was possible.

Organizations in Sverdlovsk, Moscow, and other cities began putting my name forward as a candidate in their delegations. But the apparat fought this tooth and nail, and often it had all the appearance of a farce in the tradition of the very worst years of Brezhnev's "era of stagnation." Yet everywhere *perestroika* was supposedly in full swing—after all, it was now three years since it had been officially launched.

The apparat had devised the following system: The local party organizations would put forward a large number of potential candidates; this list would then be passed up to the district committee, where many of them would be weeded out; thence it would go to the City Committee for further weeding, and finally to the provincial committee or the Central Committee of the Communist Party of the republic in question. There, behind closed doors, the list would be trimmed to only those candidates who, in the view of the apparat, would not play fast and loose at the conference but would speak and vote as they were supposed to. This system worked ideally, and the name Yeltsin was duly unseated at the very foothills of the route to the summit.

As I have already mentioned, the Muscovites showed great energy in putting my name forward at the party cells of many organizations, but even before it reached the City Committee, or at the City Committee, my candidacy was vetoed. Many party organizations in Sverdlovsk also proposed me: the Uralmash, an electrical machinery factory, the Uralkhimmash, the Verkh-Isetsk works, the Pnevnostroimashina factory, and other large enterprises. Under powerful pressure from these organizations, the Sverdlovsk City Committee decided to let my candidacy go forward. But that was not the end of it: The next stage was a plenum of the provincial committee, and there real passions flared up over the issue.

When the workers threatened to strike and the plenum still could not make the decision, the Central Committee, sensing that tension was rising fast and that the situation might get out of control, decided to retreat. At Karelia, virtually the last regional plenum in the whole country, I was elected as a delegate to the conference. My "well-wishers" could not allow me to be a delegate from Moscow or Sverdlovsk. That was why, on practically the last day of the delegate elections, I found myself in Petrozavodsk, the Karelian regional capital. At the plenum there I was warmly received, and I visited several of the local organizations. So in the end there I was, among the thirteen delegates to the Nineteenth Party Conference representing the Karelian provincial party organization.

Then several more delicate issues arose. I have already mentioned that during my political isolation, my name was taboo in the Soviet press; no such person as Yeltsin existed. Western journalists, however, were constantly asking me for interviews, and I gave one to three American television networks. I still don't understand why the Americans, when they transmitted the program, found it necessary to edit the videotape so that one of my answers was given out of context, but they did so, and it made a lot of trouble. At one of his press conferences, Gorbachev said that he would settle things with me, that I had forgotten what party discipline was, and since I was still, for the time being, a member of the Central Committee I would have to be reminded of it, or something along those lines.

Just before the start of the party conference, I was phoned, quite unexpectedly, by Aleksandr Radov, a columnist on the magazine *Ogonyok*, with the suggestion that he and I have an extensive talk, which would then be published in the magazine. Although I was pleased that one of the most popular magazines in the country (I usually read it from cover to cover) was prepared to run the risk of publishing an interview with me, I nevertheless declined the offer. "You and I will spend a long time talking to each other," I said to Radov. "You will then have to put in a lot of work editing it, and the only result will be that you won't be allowed to publish it." Radov insisted, saying that *Ogonyok* was a magazine with a lot of clout, that we would not have to show the piece to anyone, and that the editor, Valery Korotich, accepted personal responsibility for any controversial material. In the end, he persuaded me, and I agreed to give the interview. We indeed put a lot of work into it; this was to be my first appearance in the Soviet press since the October plenum, and I therefore took the opportunity very seriously. But when everything was ready for publication, a crestfallen Radov came to me and announced that the interview could not be published in *Ogonyok* after all. Korotich had decided to show it to the Central Committee, which had vetoed its publication.

I was not greatly surprised, but it did upset me. It is psychologically extremely distressing to be gagged in one's own country and to be unable to explain oneself or communicate with people except through the Western media. But most of all I was amazed when Korotich declared, in various interviews, that he had not published the conversation with me because it was not very good; I had allegedly not answered the questions that interested the magazine—in particular, I had said little about my new job—and the interview needed a lot more work. The editor in chief had decided to assume full responsibility and thereby cover up the fact that the ban had been imposed by the senior officials of the Central Committee. Why did he do this? Didn't he realize that it was immoral not to allow someone to have his say who might think differently from, for example, the general secretary? Who, if not he, a journalist, should be defending the universal principle of freedom of speech? But no, he had wriggled out of it and invented a lot of weak excuses rather than admit the real fact of the matter. If he had been afraid of the consequences, at least he could have kept his mouth shut. That would have been the more honorable course.

Thus I was feeling harassed and tense as the start of the conference approached. Every day brought something new, little of it pleasant, until I had forgotten that there was such a thing as good news.

The Nineteenth Party Conference opened in the Kremlin's Palace of Congresses. I was nervously excited as I drove to the opening session. After so many rumors, after the long conspiracy of silence, I was appearing in public for the first time, and I was well aware of the varying reactions I would encounter. A lot of curious people simply wanted to look at me, and it was these stares that irritated me most. I felt almost like an elephant in a zoo. Some of my old acquaintances averted their eyes in a cowardly fashion, in case they might be infected by this leper. I felt absolutely unnatural, almost persecuted, and tried to stay in my seat during the breaks between sessions. There were, of course, those who came up to me quite calmly, asked me how I was, and expressed their support in words, smiles, and looks.

The Karelian delegation was seated far back in the balcony. There was a space of only about six feet between our heads and the ceiling, and the presidium was barely visible. The speeches followed one after another, and as usual, some were bold and interesting but the majority were sets of ready-made clichés that had been approved in advance by the apparat.

Even so, the party conference was an important step forward. Perhaps for the first time in a party forum, delegates voted against some of the resolutions, unlike the monotonous unanimity that was the rule in the past. I had prepared a fighting speech, in which I had decided to raise the question of my political rehabilitation.

But first I had to get the right to speak. I knew that everything possible would be done to keep me away from the rostrum. The people who were organizing the conference were

221

well aware that my speech would be loaded with criticism, and they did not want to hear it.

And so, on the fifth and last day of the conference, it was announced that three speakers would have the floor before lunch; they would be proposed and voted on. That was all. I kept thinking: How am I going to speak? I sent a note to the presidium, to which there was no answer. I sent another, with the same result. When the list of speakers was read out and my name was not among them, I decided on an extreme measure. I said to my fellow members of the Karelian delegation: "Comrades, there is only one thing left for me to do. I must take the rostrum by storm." They agreed. I descended the long staircase to the doors leading straight down the center aisle to the rostrum, and I asked the KGB guards to open the doors. The officials of the KGB, who have usually treated me respectfully, flung open the double doors. I took out my red admission card, held it over my head, and strode firmly down the long aisle straight toward the presidium.

By the time I had reached the middle of that vast auditorium, everyone realized what was afoot, including the members of the presidium. The speaker—a delegate from Todjikistan, I think—broke off in the middle of his speech. A sickening deathly silence fell on the entire assembly. In that silence, with my red card held up in my outstretched hand, I walked straight forward, looking Gorbachev right in the eye. Every step reverberated within my soul. I could feel the breathing of more than five thousand people, every one of them staring at me. Reaching the presidium, I climbed the three steps, approached Gorbachev with my red card held out, and, staring at him, said in a firm voice: "I demand to be allowed to speak. Or put my request to the vote of the whole conference." There was a moment or two of confusion, but I stood my ground. Finally Gorbachev said: "Take a seat in the front row." I sat down in the front row, immediately below the rostrum, and I watched as the Politburo members held a whispered consultation. Then Gorbachev called up the head of the general department of the Central Committee, who after more whispering went out of the hall. Very soon an assistant came up to me and said: "Boris Nikolayevich, you are requested to go to the presidium's anteroom, where they would like a word with you." I inquired: "Who wants a word with me?" He replied: "I don't know," to which I replied: "No, that arrangement doesn't suit me. I shall stay here." He went away. The head of the general department returned and again conversed in whispers with the presidium, and there was more nervous movement among its members. Once again the assistant approached me, saying that one of the presidium members would come and see me in a moment or two.

I began to realize that I must not leave the hall; if I did, the doors would not be opened to me again. I said I would leave the front row but would wait in the hall to see which member of the presidium was going to talk to me. As I tiptoed back up the aisle, people in the front rows whispered to me not to leave the auditorium. I stopped three or four yards short of the exit, turned, and looked at the presidium. A group of journalists was seated near me, and they, too, advised me not to leave. I was now quite sure that I must not go out. None of the presidium members stood up. The speaker went on with his speech. The same assistant came up to me again and said that Gorbachev had promised that I would be allowed to speak but that I must first go back to the Karelian delegation. I realized that before I could get back to the gallery and return, the time for speeches would have expired and I would not be allowed to speak. So I said that I would not go back upstairs; that I had formally left the delegation and would not return; and that I preferred to sit in the front row seat that had been offered to me. I turned sharply around, went back down the aisle, and resumed my place in the front row, directly facing Gorbachev.

Had he really meant to allow me to take the rostrum, or did he conclude, on second thought, that he would lose face if he put the matter to the vote and a majority chose to allow me to speak? It is hard to say. In any event, he announced my name as a speaker, adding that after the lunch recess, the conference would proceed to the passing of resolutions.

Later, I tried to guess what might have happened if the situation had developed differently. What if the presidium had managed to persuade me to return to the gallery and the KGB man had then refused to let me back into the lower auditorium? Or if Gorbachev had exerted his authority to cut off the speeches before I had time to mount the rostrum? What then? I remain convinced that somehow or other I would have contrived to have my say, and would probably have made a direct appeal to the conference delegates, who, I felt sure, would have allowed me to speak. Even those who disliked me, who looked on me with suspicion or condemned me, had an interest in hearing what I might have to say.

So I went to the rostrum. Once again an absolute, almost oppressive, silence fell on the hall. I began to speak (here I quote the text of the stenographic record of the conference):

Comrade delegates! First of all I must respond to the questions put in his speech by Comrade Zagainov, a delegate who spoke earlier, when he touched on a number of points concerning myself.

First question: Why did I give an interview to foreign television companies and not to the Soviet press? My answer is that the first to approach me was the Soviet news agency Novosti, and I gave their reporter an interview long before I spoke to the television companies, but *Moscow News,* for which the interview was intended, was unable to publish it. Later, Novosti approached me again, but it was unable to guarantee that the interview would be published. Even before that, the magazine *Ogonyok* asked me to give them an interview; I spoke to their columnist for two whole hours, but that interview wasn't published either, even though there was an interval of six weeks between the interview and its intended date of publication. According to the statement made by Comrade Korotich, he was not allowed to print it.

Next question: Why were the remarks that I made at the organizational plenum of the Moscow City Committee so "inarticulate"? To that I can only reply that I was severely ill at the time, confined to a hospital bed without either permission or ability to get up. An hour and a half before the plenum, I was summoned to attend it, and the doctors pumped me full of the necessary drugs. I sat through the plenum, but I could understand little and was practically incapable of speech.

Further: I received a letter from the USSR State Broadcasting Committee [Gosteleradio], explaining that in connection with this conference, the committee had been given the job of coordinating all interviews with foreign television companies, and requesting that I might give an interview to several of them.

By then the number of requested interviews totaled fifteen. I told the first deputy chairman of Gosteleradio, Comrade Kravchenko, that I only had time to give interviews to two or three and no more. After that came a telephone message from Gosteleradio that three foreign television organizations had been chosen: the BBC, CBS, and ABC. I named a date and time and gave an interview to those three networks in my office. One set of questions and answers was used for all three. I refused to answer any questions that might have been detrimental to the interests or prestige of our state or party.

Some of their questions concerned my attitude toward Comrade Ligachev, and I answered that I shared his views at the strategic level, on the decisions of the Party Congress and the tasks of *perestroika*, although he and I did have certain differences of opinion on the tactics of *perestroika*, on questions of social justice, on styles of work. I did not go into detail on these points. I was also asked this question: "Do you think that if someone else had been in Comrade Ligachev's place, *perestroika* would have progressed more rapidly?" I replied: "Yes." Since my reply was taken out of context, CBS broadcast my refutation of it and sent me a written apology for the error over the signature of a vice president of the company.

I was then summoned by Comrade Solomentsev, who demanded an explanation. I expressed my indignation at being called to account and answered every question about the interview that was put to me. The attempt to pin down my guilt by reference to the party statute failed. I regard myself as completely innocent in the matter. The original videotape with the full sound track was translated for Comrade Solomentsev by our interpreter. I don't know what else may have been done to me over this business, but it reminds me strongly of shades of the recent past.

I shall now proceed to my speech.

Comrade delegates! The chief topic before this conference is the democratization of the party, bearing in mind that over time the party has become seriously deformed. In addition there is to be a discussion of today's burning questions of *perestroika* in general and of the revolutionary renewal of our society. The period of preconference preparation evoked unusual interest and hope among party members and the whole Soviet population. *Perestroika* has given our people a thorough shaking up. And it is evident that *perestroika* should have begun with a restructuring of the party itself; the party would then have drawn everyone else along behind it, as it always has done. Yet it is precisely in the matter of its own *perestroika* that the party has lagged behind. Clearly, today's conference should have been held considerably earlier. That is my personal opinion.

Even so, the preparations for the conference were rushed. The theses, compiled by the Central Committee's apparat, were published too late for discussion. No mention was made in them of the principal issue that emerged

226

in the keynote speech. Not even a majority of the Central Committee members was brought into the process of drafting the theses. It will be impossible to incorporate all the suggestions that speakers have put forward, the whole storehouse of popular wisdom, into the resolutions to be passed by our conference.

Despite Comrade Razumov's attempt in the pages of *Pravda* to convince everyone that the selection of delegates was conducted democratically, that process was conducted along the old lines by many organizations, and this demonstrated once again that the apparat of the party's upper echelon has *not* been restructured.

The discussion of ideas during the conference itself has, however, been interesting. Now the chief question is: What decisions will be made? Will they satisfy our party members and society as a whole? Judging by what happened on the first day, the impression of caution was created—I would even call it depressing. But on each subsequent day the temperature rose; the delegates' speeches become more and more interesting, and it is to be hoped that will be reflected in the resolutions that are adopted.

I would like to make a few comments and suggestions concerning the theses drawn up by the Central Committee, taking account of the speech made by Comrade Gorbachev.

On the political system, I regard it as essential that there should be a mechanism that functions, in the party and in society at large, in such a way as to exclude the repetition of errors even remotely resembling those of the past, which have set the country back several decades; a mechanism that does not create leader figures and leaderism, and that will create true popular sovereignty, backed by firm guarantees of its permanence.

The proposal, made in the chairman's keynote speech, to combine the offices of first secretary of party committees and chairmanship of the corresponding local or regional soviets was so unexpected by the delegates that one worker,

227

in his speech to the conference, said that he found it incomprehensible. Speaking as a minister, I would say: So do I. We need time to understand its implications. It is too complex a matter, and I propose that a national referendum on it should be held. [*Applause.*]

Some suggestions about the elections: They should be universal, direct, and secret, including elections to the party secretaryships, the post of general secretary of the Central Committee, and the party bureaus from top to bottom, from provincial level to the Politburo, which should be elected by all party members. This should also apply to the Supreme Soviet, the trade unions, and the Komsomol. The tenure of elective office should be limited to two terms, without exception and especially in the case of the top echelon. Officeholders should be elected for a second term solely on the basis of concrete results achieved during their preceding term. A firm upper age limit of sixty-five should be set for membership of all such bodies, including the Politburo. The length of a term of office should be calculated from the date of the previous election, and the age limit should be reckoned from the current year.

Our party, and society at large, have matured to the point where they can be trusted to decide such matters for themselves, and *perestroika* can only gain from that.

In my opinion, all these suggestions that I have made—and *not* a two-party system, as some are proposing—will be an adequate guarantee against another "cult of personality," which will not take another ten or fifteen years to emerge but can easily reappear at once if the soil is there in which it can flourish. I believe we should be on our guard against this *now*, since it has been the flouting of Leninist principles that has brought our people such calamities over recent years. Rigid barriers must be erected against it, and they must be upheld by the party statute or by the law.

In many countries it is established practice that when the leader steps down, his government steps down with him. With us, when anything goes wrong we habitually blame the dead, which is no help at all in solving our problems. It now turns out that the only person to blame for the stagnation of recent years was Brezhnev. But what about those people who were in the Politburo for ten, fifteen, or twenty years under Brezhnev—and are still in it? They voted for any program that was put before them. Why didn't they speak up when one man alone, on the basis of projects fed to him by the Central Committee's apparat, decided the fate of the party, of the country, and of socialism? They voted "yes" to the point of awarding one man his fifth star [the gold star, the medal for Hero of the Soviet Union and Hero of Socialist Labor, which Brezhnev, with Politburo compliance, awarded himself] and bringing the society as a whole to a state of crisis. Why was the ailing Chernenko promoted to the general secretaryship? Why, when it was punishing people for comparatively minor deviations from the party's standards of behavior, was the Committee of Party Control afraid to prosecute the most highly placed leaders of certain republics and provinces for bribe taking, for defrauding the state of millions of rubles? The committee was undoubtedly aware that these offenses were being committed. And it is still afraid. I must say that Comrade Solomentsev's liberal attitude to these millionaire bribe takers does make one feel a certain disquiet.

I believe that a number of members of the Politburo, as participants in the guilt of a collective body endowed with the trust of the Central Committee and the party as a whole, must answer this question: Why were the country and the party brought to the state they are in today? And after that we must draw the logical conclusion: They must be dismissed from membership in the Politburo. [Applause.] That is a more humane method than criticizing them when they are dead, digging them up and burying them all over again!

I suggest that henceforth the following procedure should be adopted: When there is a change of general secretary,

229

there should be new elections for the Politburo, except for those who have recently been elected to it; and broadly speaking, the personnel of the Central Committee's apparat should also be changed. Then the nation will not be trapped by a permanent, unchanging administration. Then people will no longer be criticized only after their death, knowing as they will that every one of them, including every member of the elective element of the Central Committee, is answerable to the party at large.

Further: At present, despite the general secretary's clear statement that no areas of policy and no leaders—including himself—are immune to criticism, in reality this is not the case. There is an area, a dividing line, above which, from the first hint of criticism, there is an instant warning: "Hands off!" The result is that even members of the Central Committee are afraid to express their personal opinions to the leadership if the opinion differs from an official statement of policy.

This does the greatest possible harm. It distorts an individual's personality and his party conscience, and it trains him into the habit of instantly raising his hand with the "ayes"—along with everyone else—whenever a vote is called for, no matter what the issue may be. The present conference is, I believe, the first exception to what has become the rule. Until now it has been the case that the policies carried out by the leading party bodies have remained immune to criticism and beyond check or scrutiny by the mass of the people.

We must concur with the proposal in Comrade Gorbachev's keynote speech to create a commission, drawn from members of the Central Committee, to set long-term policy guidelines and to ensure that without the scrutiny and approval of this commission not a single Central Committee resolution or directive may be put into effect. Now such directives are the work of not the Central Committee but its bureaucratic apparat, and many of them are never implemented. Major projects should be discussed by the whole party and by the country at large, including the holding of referendums. As a rule, the practice of issuing decrees jointly by the Central Committee and the USSR Council of Ministers should be abolished.

Yes, we are proud of socialism and proud of what has been achieved, but we must not rest on our laurels. In seventy years, after all, we have not yet solved the main problems: how to feed and clothe the population, how to ensure an efficient service sector of the economy, and how to resolve social problems. It is the aim of *perestroika* to tackle all these, but its progress is being seriously held back, which means that each one of us is not putting enough vigor into working for it and fighting for it. But it is also true that one of the main obstacles to *perestroika* is the way it was brought into being. It was announced without adequate analysis of the causes of the stagnation that preceded it, without analysis of the current state of society, without a profound historical analysis of the party's shortcomings and past errors. As a result, after three years of *perestroika* we have not solved any of the real problems experienced by ordinary people, and still less have we achieved any revolutionary transformations.

In putting *perestroika* into effect, we should set our sights not only on the year 2000 (to many people it is a matter of no importance whether they get anything then or what they may get) but also on each successive period of two or three years ahead, and within each period we should finally solve one or two specific problems for the good of the people. Without dissipating our efforts in other directions, we should concentrate everything—resources, science, human energy—on tackling those selected issues. Then— encouraged by a rapidly increasing faith that the restructuring of society is really under way, that it works, that it is irreversible—people will resolve other problems at a significantly faster rate. As things are, people's faith in *perestroika* is likely to waver at any moment. So far, they are all still hypnotized by words, and that has saved the situation.

For the future, however, there is a risk of losing both direction and political stability.

Now about openness in the party: A variety of opinions should be the normal state of affairs, rather than colorless, standardized thinking. The existence of a distinct minority opinion will not destroy but only strengthen the unity of the party. The party exists for the people, and the people should know what the party is doing. This, unfortunately, does not happen. Detailed accounts of the proceedings of the Politburo and the Central Committee secretariat should be available, with the exception of topics involving state secrets. The public should also know about the lives and achievements of its leaders—what they do, what salaries they receive, and the results achieved by each member of the top echelon in the sector for which he is responsible. There should also be regular appearances on television, announcements of the results of the entry of new members into the party, summaries of workers' letters addressed to the Central Committee, and so on. In general, there should be a comprehensive sociology to examine the moral health of the leaders of the party and the state. It should be open to all and not kept secret.

And then there are the forbidden, secret topics such as the details of the party's budget. It is stated in the party statutes that the Central Committee decides on the expenditure of party funds—not just the apparat's but the whole party's. But financial matters are not discussed at the plenary sessions of the Central Committee. I suggest that henceforth this should be compulsory, because neither the members of the Central Committee nor still less other party members know anything about how the party's funds are spent—and they amount to hundreds of millions of rubles. The audit commission never reports on this at party congresses; indeed, the commission is not even allowed access to the books.

I know, for instance, exactly how many millions of rubles are transferred to the Central Committee from the Moscow city and Sverdlovsk provincial party organizations. But how they are spent—I have no idea. I can only observe that apart from rational and necessary expenditures, the party spends its money on building luxurious houses, dachas, and sanatoriums on such a scale as to make one ashamed when representatives of other socialist parties visit. That money should instead be used for the material support of the primary grass-roots party organizations, including the payment of decent salaries to their leading officials.

We are surprised when certain senior party leaders besmirch themselves with corruption, bribery, and secret additions to their salaries; when they lose all sense of decency, moral purity, modesty, and comradely relations with other party members. The corruption of the upper levels of the party under Brezhnev spread to many regions, and we must not overlook or condone this. The rottenness has surely gone deeper than many people suppose, and as I know from my experience in Moscow, the mafia most definitely exists.

I now turn to matters of social justice. In broad outline, of course, we have dealt with these questions of socialist principles. But several problems remain unsolved, which arouse people's indignation, lower the party's authority, and have the most dire effect on the tempo of *perestroika*.

In my opinion, the principle should be as follows: If there is a lack of anything in our socialist society, then that shortage should be felt in equal degree by everyone without exception. *[Applause.]* Differences in individual contributions to society in terms of labor should be reflected by differential payment; we must, at last, abolish the special "rations" of otherwise unobtainable foods given to the "starving" party establishment; we must eliminate elitism in our society, eliminate in both word and deed the epithet "special" from our vocabulary, since there are no such creatures as "special" Communists.

I believe this will greatly help party officials to work with the rest of the population and will also help *perestroika*.

Now a few words about the structure and reduction in size of the party apparat. Lenin's call "All Power to the Soviets!" will never be realized given the existence of such a massive party apparat. I propose that we reduce the apparat of provincial committees by two or three times, of the Central Committee by between six and ten times, including the abolition of those departments that at present deal with the various branches of the economy.

I would also like to mention young people. There is practically nothing about them in the theses for discussion at this conference. A lot was said about them, however, in the keynote speech, and I would support the proposal to pass a separate resolution on young people. For it is they, and not we, who will have to play the main part in renewing our socialist society. We must boldly teach them how to redirect this process at all levels and hand over whole areas of leadership to them.

Comrade delegates! I now come to a ticklish matter. I would like to raise the question of my personal political rehabilitation after the October 1987 plenum of the Central Committee. [Noise in the hall.] If you think that time will not permit it, then I have finished my remarks.

GORBACHEV: Speak on, Boris Nikolayevich. They want you to have your say. [Applause.] I think we should stop treating the Yeltsin case as secret. Let Boris Nikolayevich say whatever he thinks necessary. And if you and I feel the need, then we, too, can say a word or two after he has spoken. Go ahead, Boris Nikolayevich!

YELTSIN: Comrade delegates! Rehabilitation fifty years after a person's death has now become the rule, and this has had a healthy effect on society. But I am asking for my personal political rehabilitation while I am still alive. I regard this as a matter of principle and very appropriate, in light of the calls made, in the keynote speech and in delegates' speeches, for socialist pluralism of opinions, for freedom to criticize, and for tolerance toward opponents.

You know that by a decision of the Central Committee

234

my speech at the October 1987 plenum of the Central Committee was declared to be politically erroneous. But the questions that were raised at the plenum have since been raised on more than one occasion by the press and by party members. In the last few days practically all those same questions were asked from this very rostrum, both in the keynote speech and in delegates' speeches. I consider that the only error in my speech was that I delivered it at the wrong time—immediately before the seventieth anniversary of the October Revolution.

Clearly, we all need to master the rules of political discussion, to tolerate dissenting opinions as Lenin did; not to hang labels on people and not to regard them as heretics.

Comrade delegates! In the speeches made at this conference, including my own, the same questions that I raised at the October 1987 plenum have been fully aired. I resent what happened there very keenly, and I request that the conference withdraw the resolution about me which was passed at that plenum. If you consider it possible to annul it, you will thereby rehabilitate me in the eyes of party members. It is not only something personal; it will be in the spirit of *perestroika.* It will be democratic, and I believe it will help the cause of *perestroika* by increasing popular confidence in the party.

It is certainly proving hard to renew our society. But certain fundamental shifts, though small, have taken place, and life itself obliges us to take that road and no other. *[Applause.]*

I finished my speech. To some degree, my extreme tension had hampered me, but even so I believe I kept myself and my nervous excitement under control and I said everything I had to say and wanted to say. The reaction to my speech was good; at least they were applauding until I left the lower auditorium and started upstairs to the balcony, where I rejoined the Karelian delegation. Just then the lunch recess was announced. Some fellow delegates showed me the warmest at-

235

tention, while others conveyed their support with a smile or a handshake. I was keyed up and tense. I went outside, where I was surrounded by delegates and journalists who asked me endless questions.

Suspecting nothing, I went back to my delegation after the break. According to the rules of procedure, the conference was supposed to start voting on resolutions and other decisions. But it turned out that the break had been used to mount a counterattack on me and my speech from a whole battery of guns.

Ligachev's speech was memorable. Subsequently it was to be recycled in jokes, comedy sketches, and satirical cartoons. The text even had to be corrected for grammar and syntax in the published stenographic transcript, otherwise the Soviet Union's chief ideologist would have looked incompetent. Despite all the labels he hung on me, despite all the nonsense he invented about me, and despite all his furious efforts, the whole thing was petty, vulgar, and illiterate.

It was after that speech, I believe, that his political career started to wane. He dealt himself such a crushing blow that he will never be able to recover from it. After the party conference he should have submitted his resignation, but he didn't want to. He didn't want to, but he will have to do so all the same. Since that speech, which reduced many delegates to embarrassed laughter, there is nothing else for him to do.

The next speech was given by Lukin, the young first secretary of Moscow's Proletarsky district committee. He diligently showered me with mud, carrying out the noble task set him by the leadership. I have often wondered how he could go on living with his conscience after that. In the end, I decided that he would continue to get on splendidly with his conscience, because it has become so hardened. When these young careerists start climbing upward, they have to tell so many lies and do such things that in a case like his it is better not to mention his conscience at all.

236

Then came Chikiryov, general manager of the Ordzhonikidze works. It was he who, in addition to spreading many other lies about me, concocted the story about the first secretary who allegedly threw himself out of a seventh-story window on my account. As I listened to him I was not sure whether I was awake or having a nightmare. I had been to his factory and had once even spent a whole day there with a minister, Panichev. As always, I had spent some time in the canteen and the workers' rest rooms, and after the visit I had made some comments, with which he appeared to agree. And now, suddenly, he poured out such invective against me that it is unrepeatable—nothing but lies and distortions of the facts. As may be imagined, this reduced me to a state of deep depression.

Then, to everyone's complete surprise, V. A. Volkov, a delegate from Sverdlovsk, came up to the rostrum and spoiled the scenario by saying a lot of kind words about me. I had never met Volkov before then. His sincere, impulsive speech was a natural human reaction to blatant injustice. But after a few minutes the terrified first secretary of the Sverdlovsk provincial committee, Bobykin, sent a note up to the presidium. I will quote it: "The delegation of the Sverdlovsk provincial party organization fully supports the decision made by the October 1987 plenum of the Central Committee with regard to Comrade Yeltsin. No one empowered Comrade Volkov to speak in the name of our delegates. His speech has been thoroughly condemned. In the name of the Sverdlovsk delegation: Bobykin, first secretary, provincial committee." In fact, he did not consult his delegation before writing that note.

In conclusion Gorbachev also had plenty to say about me, but at least his remarks were not so crude and unrestrained.

All those around me were afraid even to turn and look at me. I sat motionless, staring down at the rostrum from the balcony, feeling that at any moment I might lose consciousness. Noticing my condition, several of the young stewards on duty took me to a doctor, who gave me an injection to enable me at least to hold out and stay in place until the end of the conference. I returned to my seat, but it was physical and moral agony. I felt as if I were on fire inside, and everything was swimming in front of my eyes.

I found it very hard to recover from it all. I did not sleep for two nights in a row, agonizing and wondering: What is happening? Who is right and who is wrong? This, I felt, was the end. There was no other forum in which I could defend and justify myself. The session of the Nineteenth Party Conference had been transmitted by television, live and in full, to the whole country. I felt that the establishment was satisfied; they had beaten me to the ground, and they had won. At that moment I was overcome by apathy.

Letters began to arrive from all over the country, from its most distant corners. Many of those who wrote reproached me about only one thing—that in my speech to the conference I had asked to be politically rehabilitated. "Didn't you know what sort of people most of these delegates were and how the delegate elections were carried out?" they asked me. "How could you ask anything of these people?" One man—I think he was an engineer from Leningrad—wrote: "Even Woland, the diabolical figure in Bulgakov's *The Master and Margarita*, said that one should never ask favors of anyone. And you forgot that sacred rule."

Still, I believe I was right to put the matter of my political rehabilitation to the delegates. It was important to state my position and to say out loud that the resolution of the October plenum of the Central Committee that declared my speech to be a grave political error was in itself a political error and should be withdrawn. I had no great illusions that this might happen, but I still had hope.

In the end, it was the people who affirmed my true rehabilitation. At the election of people's deputies, nearly ninety percent of the Moscow electorate voted for me. That was the most important form of rehabilitation, more precious to me than any other. Whether or not the resolution of the October plenum is ever withdrawn, it no longer has any significance for me. The issue is of much greater importance for Gorbachev himself and for the Central Committee.

I didn't want to do any more fighting, any more explaining. I just wanted to forget everything, if only they would leave me in peace. But most of the letters offered support. It was a fantastic demonstration. People suggested honey, herbs, raspberry jam, and massage to build up my strength and prevent me from ever falling ill again. I was advised to pay no attention to the idiotic things that had been said about me, since nobody believed them anyway. I was urged not to lose heart but to go on fighting for *perestroika*.

I received so many kind, touching, warm letters from total strangers that I kept asking myself: Where does it come from, why do they write, and for what reason? I did, of course, understand exactly where those burningly sincere emotions were coming from—our long-suffering people simply could not stand by calmly and watch dispassionately as a man was being pilloried. People were incensed by the obvious, clear injustice of it. In sending me those encouraging letters they were holding out their hands to me, and I was able to lean on them to get on my feet again.

And to go forward once more.

9

March 27, 1989

Chronicle of the Election Campaign

It is all over. The months-long marathon is finished. I don't know which is the stronger feeling—exhaustion or relief.

I have been told the precise results of the election: 89.6 percent of the electorate voted for me. This is not quite a normal figure—in a more civilized election, the number of votes for me should have been lower; but here people had been brought to such a state and such efforts had been made to discredit me, tell lies about me, and prevent my election that I might well have collected even more votes.

Recently a new excuse for my success has been circulated:

People didn't vote for Yeltsin; they voted against apparat. It is assumed that this remark will offend me, but I find it gratifying if it means that my unequal struggle against the party bureaucracy was not fought in vain. If a protest against the apparat is associated with the name of Yeltsin, then there was some justification for my speeches at the October 1987 plenum of the Central Committee and at the Nineteenth Party Conference.

I very much want to stop, look around me, and have a rest; the election campaign has been so wearing and exhausting. But it's not possible; new problems and worries are already overwhelming me.

I have written a formal request to N. I. Ryzhkov, chairman of the USSR Council of Ministers, asking him to release me from my ministerial post. According to the election law, a people's deputy cannot simultaneously be a minister, so as of today I am officially unemployed.

I have had telephone calls from Sverdlovsk congratulating me and saying that several progressive deputies were elected from their province, while Bobykin, the first secretary of the provincial party committee, was crushingly defeated. What's more, he had run in a remote and, as he imagined, docile rural district, from which all other potential candidates had been eliminated at the nominating meeting. Yet even so the voters have thrown him out.

Meanwhile here at home the telephone has been ringing every minute. There have been hundreds of calls, all congratulating me, wishing me luck, and sending the warmest greetings. Naya and I have arranged to leave Moscow for a few weeks and go someplace where we can hide from everyone.

I am, in fact, extremely tired and need a rest.

I sometimes feel that I have lived three different lives. The first, although not without its difficulties and tensions, was

242

much like other people's lives—study, work, family, a career as an industrial manager and then as a party official. It ended on the day of the October 1987 plenum of the Central Committee. Then began my second life—as a political outcast, surrounded by a void, a vacuum. I found myself cut off from people and had to struggle to survive, both as a human being and as a politician. Then, on the day I won the election as a people's deputy, my third life began—my third birth, so to speak. Less than a year has passed since then. And while little was known about the first two stages of my life, everything that has happened since the election—my work in the Congress of People's Deputies and at sessions of the Supreme Soviet, the creation of the Inter-Regional Group of Deputies, my trip to the U.S.A., attempts to compromise me—has taken place in public. There have been no secrets and no blank pages. But since so many events have been crammed into these months, I must describe them.

After my resounding victory at the polls, rumors were circulating that when the Congress of People's Deputies met, I would challenge Gorbachev for the post of chairman of the Supreme Soviet. I don't know how those rumors arose— whether from my supporters, who were in a state of euphoria after my election, or among my enemies, frightened by such a powerful reaction from the voters of Moscow—but the rumors stubbornly persisted.

What did I feel about this? Practically nothing. I had a wholly realistic view of the political situation in the country, and I had made a fairly exact prediction of the strength of the minority and majority in the Congress of People's Deputies, so that I had no illusions or ambitions on that score. I was, however, aware that my presence in the Congress would worry Gorbachev and that he would want to know my intentions.

About a week before the opening session, he phoned me and suggested that we meet for a talk. The meeting lasted about an hour. For the first time in a long while we sat face-to-face. The conversation was tense and nervous, and I revealed to him much of the anxiety that had built up inside me over the past months. My own problems worried me least of all; what horrified me was that the country was falling apart. The bureaucracy was playing the same old games, keeping all power within its own hands and not allowing a scrap of it to pass to the Congress of People's Deputies. I kept on trying to probe for the heart of his position: Was he with the people—or with the system that had brought the country to the brink of disaster?

His answers were brusque and harsh, and the longer we talked, the thicker grew the wall between us. When it became obvious that no human contact was going to be made, that no relationship of mutual trust could be built up, Gorbachev modified the tone and intensity of his remarks and asked about my plans for the future. What was I going to do, what sort of work did I see myself taking up? I replied straight away that the Congress would decide everything. Gorbachev did not like that answer. He wanted me to give him some kind of guarantee, so he went on questioning me. What did I think of a job in industry? Would I be interested in a seat on the Council of Ministers? But I stuck to my line: The Congress would decide everything. I think I was right to do so; it was pointless to talk seriously about another job before the Congress had even started its work; but my reply irritated Gorbachev. He wanted to know more precisely about my intentions, and he obviously thought I was concealing something from him. But I was quite sincere about not having made any plans; only after the session of the Congress would it be possible to start thinking about the future. On that we parted.

The very next day, new rumors were being spread around Moscow. Oh, where is the poet or bard who will compose an ode to Russian rumors? Thanks to the chronic shortage of truthful (or even false) information, our people live on ru-mors. They constitute the most important telegraphic agency of the Soviet Union, of far greater importance than Tass it-self. One would like to think that one day someone will make a study of our rumor mill—how rumors arise and how they are circulated. It would make a fascinating book. This time the rumors announced that Gorbachev had met Yeltsin and offered him the post of first deputy prime minister, which Yeltsin had refused because he wanted to be chairman of the Supreme Soviet. This refusal had then forced Gorbachev to offer him the office of first deputy chairman of the Supreme Soviet, but Yeltsin had again refused—to which Gorbachev had responded with an offer of the position of first secretary of the Moscow City Committee of the Party . . . and this Yeltsin had accepted.

Several people passed this story on to me, or variations of it. One could only shake one's head and marvel at the fertility of the human imagination.

Soon after that the Congress opened. I shall say very little about it, because anyone who was interested has been able to follow its progress in minutest detail. Gorbachev made the important decision that the entire session should be broad-cast, live, on national television. Those ten days, in which almost the whole country watched the desperate debates of the Congress, unable to tear themselves away from their tele-vision sets, gave the people more of a political education than seventy years of stereotyped Marxist-Leninist lectures multi-plied a millionfold and flung at the Soviet people in order to turn them into dummies. On the day the Congress opened, they were one sort of people; on the day that it closed, they were different people. However negatively we may assess the results of the Congress of People's Deputies, however much pain and regret we may have felt at the missed opportunities, the political and economic measures that were *not* taken in the right direction—nonetheless, the most important thing was achieved: Almost the entire population was awakened from its state of lethargy.

As usual, it did not pass off without some tense moments for me. During the discussions on the method of choosing the members of the new Supreme Soviet from among the people's deputies, I insisted categorically that this process should be a contested election. I honestly admit to hoping with all my heart that I would be elected to the Supreme Soviet, although I also realized quite soberly that this particular body of people's deputies might well decide otherwise. The silent and obedient majority, which we had inherited from the recent past, would squash any proposal that displeased the leadership. And so it was. The first few votes cast showed how successfully Gorbachev was managing to manipulate the Congress, and the elections to the Supreme Soviet only confirmed the fact that the cast-iron majority would block the path of anyone who was likely to step out of line. Sakharov, Chernichenko, Popov, Shmeylov, Zaslavskaya—all of them excellent, respected, and highly competent deputies—failed to be elected to the Supreme Soviet. There were indeed so many who were *not* elected that it would be impossible to list them all. And I was among them. More than half the deputies voted for me, but I was still obliged to give way to those of my colleagues who received more votes than I did. I was not disturbed by this. I am not saying that to show how stoical I was; the result was to be expected. If that particular Congress membership had voted me into the Supreme Soviet, it would have greatly surprised me. Events had taken their natural course, and I waited with interest to see how Gorbachev would wriggle out of the situation he had created for himself.

It was, of course, a scandal. Everyone realized that because of me this state of affairs might ultimately become explosive. The voters of Moscow regarded the outcome of the elections to the Supreme Soviet as a crass disregard of the wishes of several million people. That evening there began a series of spontaneous meetings, and here and there calls were heard for a political strike.

As always in Soviet conditions, an individual emerged who had the sense to find a way out of this impasse. On this occasion the person who saved the situation was Yuri Kazannik, a deputy from Siberia. He was elected to the Supreme Soviet but withdrew his candidacy in my favor. The Congress was obliged to approve this "castling" move; when hands were raised in the Congress hall and Gorbachev saw that the substitution would be approved, his face showed a look of unconcealed relief.

Thus I became a member of the Supreme Soviet of the USSR, and the question of my future employment became redundant. A few days later I was elected chairman of the Supreme Soviet's Committee on Construction and Architecture, and thus, ex officio, I also became a member of the Presidium of the Supreme Soviet of the USSR.

I could spend a long time describing the proceedings of the Congress, which were marked by numerous dramatic, thrilling, and tense situations. The whole country witnessed these events on television, as did the rest of the world, which is by no means indifferent to what goes on in one-sixth of the inhabited globe. Therefore I will not dwell on these episodes, for life has moved on again since then.

Generally speaking, the nearly two months' work of the session of the Supreme Soviet, which included organizing the Committee on Construction and Architecture from zero, was marked by our traditional chaotic disorder—no offices for us to work in, no rooms in which to receive our constituents, incomprehensible instructions concerning a deputy's secretary or assistant, the dictatorship of the Supreme Soviet's permanent staff over the deputies. We will learn; at the moment

247

we are still in the infants' class of the great parliamentary school, and I think it will take a long time before we reach university level.

Among the key episodes of the summer of 1989 was the miners' strike, which rocked the whole country. The day of the intimidated, obedient, puppetlike Soviet working class is past, and I would like to believe it is gone forever. A completely different worker has now stepped into the political arena—a worker who respects both himself and the value of his labor. As before, there are plenty of frightened, weary people who regard their bosses with fear and trembling, but every day there are more of the other kind: men and women who have straightened their shoulders and hold their heads high. It was these workers who headed the strike committees and were followed by tens of thousands of their fellow miners.

Moscow's reaction was swift and precise. For a few days, the newspapers described the strikers' demands in the usual tone of irritated disapproval, then suddenly, all at once, in every forum and in the columns of every newspaper, there was total support for the miners' position. Naturally, if the strike had occurred in only one region, the reaction would have been the reverse, but the fact that all the miners in the country managed to unite determined the success of the strike.

Unfortunately, Ryzhkov and his new team of ministers proved unable fully to exploit this situation. He had a real chance to break the backbone of our bureaucratically run command economy. Both the Supreme Soviet and public opinion were ready to accept radical economic reforms. But once again half-measures were proposed, again it ended up as an attempt to solve the problems of only one branch of industry.

Another very important event, in which I took an active part, was the formation of the Inter-Regional Group of Deputies.

I believe that July 29–30, 1989, will go down in the history of Soviet society. It was then, in the House of the Cinema in Moscow, that the IRGD first met. The epoch of monolithic unity was brought to an end. In spite of unprecedented pressure put on the deputies to convince them that there was no place in the numerous halls of the Kremlin for such a meeting to be held, in spite of the attempt to label us schismatics, splitters, dictators, and so on—the words of abuse were unending—we nevertheless gathered.

Why did we have to do it? Because what is happening to our country borders on catastrophe. The situation cannot be saved by half-measures and timid steps. Only decisive, radical measures can drag us back from the abyss. Everything that progressive deputies had announced in their electoral platforms, all the best ideas for getting us out of the blind alley, were combined in the program and platform of the IRGD. Elections were held to choose five cochairmen of the group; Sakharov and I were among them.

I don't want to theorize in this book, but perhaps the time has come to indicate, even if only in a few words, the program for which I stand and which is shared by many of the deputies who have joined the IRGD.

There are not many points of principle that divide the so-called rightists and leftists of the group. No doubt the main one is the question of property. If one accepts the private ownership of property, then this means the collapse of the main buttress that supports the state's monopoly of property ownership and everything that stems from it: the power of the state, the alienation of the state from the individual and his labor, and so on. The second point in our program is probably less important: the land question. The slogan "Land to the Peasants" is now even more relevant than it was seventy-odd years ago. Only when the land is worked by the people who own it will the country be fed. Next is the decentralization of power, the economic independence of the republics

249

and their genuine sovereignty—this will go far toward solving the country's ethnic problems. We also call for the elimination of all structural and financial limitations to the economic independence of enterprises and labor collectives. There must be a reform of the country's financial situation, which is directly linked to the measures referred to above (e.g., the proposals concerning property, land, and regional independence), although special financial measures must also be taken to prevent the complete collapse of the ruble. I will not go into any greater detail on this point. The IRGD contains several first-class economists, who have drawn up a list of vitally urgent measures needed to save the country's finances. Yet their advice is not being followed.

Why have I always been one of those who have not responded to the calls for immediate adoption of a multiparty system? Because the mere existence of several parties does not in itself solve any problems. Several parties existed in Czechoslovakia and the German Democratic Republic, but until very recently the socialism in those countries was of the Brezhnev-Stalin brand, though with certain specific local features. There are also several parties, by the way, in North Korea.

My view is that we still need to grow and mature toward a real, civilized, multiparty system. One other comment on this topic. We do not have several parties, but it is an illusion to think that we have one party, united and unbeatable. In actual fact, if the party leadership can include Yuri Afanasiev and Viktor Afanasiev; Yeltsin and Ligachev; a deputy named Samsonov and a deputy named Vlasov, a former weight lifter —all poles apart in their political positions and their actions —it means that our concepts have become completely muddled and we have altogether forgotten what a political party is. As a matter of urgency, I suggest that we pass a new law on the party, giving legal force to a situation in which the party is a part of *society* and not of the *state*, and guaranteeing that citizens are free to combine in social organizations and parties. We should also delete Article 6 from the Constitution, which legitimizes the Communist Party's monopoly of power.

Another important issue is the relationship between church and state. Stalin succeeded in creating the only state in the world in which even the church was brought to its knees and subordinated to it. Only now, and with great difficulty, has the church begun to recover consciousness after the crushing blows delivered to it over many decades. The facts of the recent past that we can now read in the press—such as how priests informed on their parishioners to the party authorities and the KGB—bear witness not to the degeneration of the church but to the fact that when a society is sick, all its limbs become unhealthy too. Today the church has begun to recover its health, and I am convinced that the moment is coming when, with its message of eternal, universal values, it will come to the aid of our society. For in these words: Thou shalt not kill; Thou shalt love thy neighbor as thyself, lie those very moral principles that will enable us to survive even the most critical situations. The principle of freedom of conscience is written into our Constitution, but we know only too well how that principle has been observed in practice. And that article of the Constitution will remain a dead letter until the economic and political reform of our country has been made a reality, until the worth of the human individual becomes the paramount value in our society. At present the opposite prevails: The paramount value of our system of rule by the party bureaucracy is the state. And we have to serve the state. I hope—at least I am doing and will do everything I can to this end—that it is only a matter of months, weeks, days before that service to the state comes to an end.

Now a word about the KGB, the army, and the Ministry of Internal Affairs, which controls the police and a large contingent of special troops. Here, of course, the situation is more or less clear. These organizations have always been the bulwark of state power. In totalitarian systems, their role and power are constantly being increased. The wind of change has not touched any of them; on the contrary, to everyone's surprise, Kryuchkov, the chairman of the KGB, was suddenly allowed to bypass the stage of candidate member of the Politburo and was immediately made a full member. This revival of the old tradition by merging the party leadership with the security organization naturally shocked everyone. In a time of *perestroika* and *glasnost*, if only out of tact and common sense, Gorbachev should not have turned one of the state committees into the senior and most important committee. But no; the thirst for power and the fear of losing it are stronger than any logic or common sense. The KGB has to be close at hand to stand guard over the party's interests, so let Kryuchkov be one of the "inner circle."

I can foresee that a fierce, hard struggle lies ahead over the future of the army and the KGB. We have not even begun to consider reforming these most important structures in the edifice of the state. And the reason is that we lack the strength to do so. It has become an almost unconscious reflex to jump to attention at the very mention of the words "army" or "KGB"—just in case. The feeling of fear lives in practically every Soviet citizen. This is why the leadership of both the army and the KGB quite calmly and, I would say, unceremoniously ignore the demands by deputies to decode the secret budgets of these organizations. They are not prepared to reveal any details of the activities and structure of these forces, and without such knowledge all talk of restructuring and limiting their functions, of reducing their size and role, is so much hot air.

What do I hope for? First—and most important—I am relying on the development of society itself. Clearly, the KGB and the armed forces are always going to lag behind in reforming themselves, but they are also going to have to adapt to the processes that are taking place in the country, and they will be obliged to keep up with them.

Second, I am putting my hopes on the men themselves. The army and the KGB are manned not by lead soldiers but by living people. A new generation of recruits, now being taken into the armed services, will protest against the old image of the "brutal and licentious soldiery," against blind obedience, against the lack of professionalism, and against accepting the old ways.

The salvation of both the army and the KGB will be *glasnost*, openness. And every one of us who values *perestroika* will fight for this. As for the future of these forces, there is no need to invent anything new. Other societies have already developed smoothly functioning mechanisms for a proper relationship with the army and the security organization, in which they are not above society but *serve* society and are subordinate to parliament. The army, in my view, must become a professional, volunteer force. Only then can it be improved—but I am starting to go into detail.

I have moved far away from the story of the Inter-Regional Group of Deputies, and will now return to it because it is very instructive. While the coordinating council of the IRGD was meeting in the rare hours that we could snatch from our spare time, and while we were giving ourselves brainstorms in the attempt to put together a set of programs that would offer the country a way out of the crisis, a storm of a quite different nature blew up: an organized attempt to discredit members of the group. In the newspapers, at constituency meetings, at local party meetings, on every possible and impossible occasion, people were told that they—that is, we—were greedy for power; that we wanted to subject the country to a dictatorship; that we were an opposition; that we were a clique of intellectuals and bureaucrats remote from the people; that most of us had obscure and shady pasts.

Once again, and not for the first time in Soviet political life, an attempt was being made to substitute for the process of dialogue, of comparing different views and attitudes—a process natural and necessary for a society that has renounced the artificial state of total unanimity—personal attacks on the people who supported and expressed those views and attitudes.

All this has happened before in our history and has brought the Soviet people nothing but incalculable hardship and suffering. It is time to realize that our society—fortunately—is *not* homogeneous; that its different social groupings and strata have different interests, which do not altogether coincide.

It is time to realize that the Inter-Regional Group of Deputies is not "a collection of ambitious, power-hungry politicians." We express the interests of that significant proportion of our society which believes that *perestroika* is not being practiced consistently and firmly enough, that our present troubles are *not* caused by trying to cure "good" socialism with a dose of "bad" capitalism. In encountering the first difficulties in the process of reforming our brand of bureaucratized "barracks socialism," we have tried to find solutions by the use of the same old methods of the bureaucratic state and the "command economy."

But the main objective has nevertheless been achieved. The group exists and is working out the strategies and tactics needed to develop our society anew. Since it includes the best brains among the deputies, there will ultimately be no alternative: The people will follow the lead of the Inter-Regional Group of Deputies.

After the IRGD finished the first stage of its work, there was a short parliamentary recess, and in mid-September I went to America. That short trip, lasting no more than eight days, caused a considerable stir.

I visited the United States at the request of several American organizations and universities and a number of politicians; altogether I received fifteen invitations. The trip was originally meant to last for two weeks, but the Central Committee would let me go for only one week. This was a disaster for the people who were organizing my visit, and they asked me not to disrupt the schedule but to try to fit most of the planned engagements and lectures into a single week. At school and later at the polytechnic, I had studied Marx's theory of the exploitation of man by man under capitalism. I now experienced that indisputable theory being applied to myself. Sleeping for only two or three hours a day, I flew from one state to another, attended meetings or made speeches six or seven times a day, without letup for a week, during which I visited nine states and eleven cities. After running that marathon at the pace of a dash, I came to my senses only on the plane returning me to Moscow, and it is now my dream to go back to America, but this time to see it not as in a speeded-up film but calmly and without haste, so that I can examine those details of the country for which on my first trip there was no time to spare.

A great deal has been written about my trip to America, both there and in the Soviet Union, so I doubt whether it is worth dwelling on the overall results of the journey. I met with many interesting people, from President Bush to ordinary Americans on the streets of those eleven cities. No doubt it will sound banal, but what surprised me most were precisely those ordinary people in America, who radiated optimism and faith in themselves and in their country. There were, of course, shattering experiences of another sort—the supermarkets, for example. When I saw those shelves crammed with hundreds, thousands of cans, cartons, and goods of every possible sort, for the first time I felt quite frankly sick with despair for the Soviet people. That such a potentially superrich country as ours has been brought to a state of such poverty! It is terrible to think of it.

Under the terms agreed in advance with the organizers of

255

my trip, I was paid fees for the lectures that I gave at universities. On the last day, it turned out that after deducting all the expenses covering the costs of our four-man group, the sum remaining at my disposal was $100,000. I decided to contribute that money to the Soviet anti-AIDS campaign by acquiring a consignment of single-use hypodermic syringes, and only a week later the first shipment of 100,000 syringes arrived in Moscow for distribution to eleven children's hospitals. The total order was for a million syringes, which accounted for the money down to the last cent.

I raise this because at the very moment when I was signing the document ordering my American earnings to be spent on those syringes, the first morning editions of *Pravda* were going on sale in Moscow's kiosks with an article reprinted from the Italian newspaper *La Repubblica*. It reported that throughout my time in America I had been hopelessly drunk. The journalist even quoted the exact quantities of what I had allegedly drunk during the whole trip (although here the Italian's imagination had clearly failed him; only a weak-headed foreigner could have been brought to his knees by those amounts of alcohol). It also appeared that the Moscow hospitals would have to wait in vain for the syringes, because I was alleged to have spent all my money on video recorders and videocassettes, on presents for myself, consisting of suits, white shirts, shoes, and other finery; that I hardly ever emerged from a series of supermarkets, where I had nothing to say but "I'll have that . . . and that . . . and that!" The article (translated and published by *Pravda* with uncharacteristic speed) made me look like the usual drunken, lumbering, ill-mannered Russian bear at his first encounter with civilized society.

I had known, of course, that my trip would provoke a fiercely negative reaction from the top level of the Soviet establishment. I had suspected that there would be attempts to compromise me and discredit my visit to the U.S.A. But I had not expected that my detractors would stoop so low and descend to such stupid and boldfaced lies.

The reaction of the Muscovites and many, many people all over the country was unanimous. I received thousands of telegrams of support. Another provocation had failed in its aim.

But my invisible opponents did not let it rest at that. Shortly thereafter, a ninety-minute program about my U.S. trip was shown on central television, preceded by something very rare—a preliminary trailer on "Vremya," the main current affairs program. And the chief item on the program, the reason for the whole elaborate setup, was my meeting with students and faculty members at Johns Hopkins University.

I have already mentioned that in America I was subjected to an insane timetable, which, added to the change of time zones, exhaustion, and lack of sleep, led me, after a night flight, to take a sedative. I immediately fell asleep, only to be awakened two hours later, at six in the morning: There was another official meeting at seven, and at eight I had to make a speech at Johns Hopkins. Still completely knocked out, I felt that I could not get up and asked to postpone the meeting. I was told that was impossible; there would be a scandal, which my hosts would never survive. I said that I would not survive the day. Still, weak as I was, I summoned up all my willpower and attended the first meeting, then the second. I gradually felt better. The enforced movement helped me to overcome my fatigue, and the effect of the pill also wore off. Well, precisely that episode, of the dozens that could have been put on the air, was shown to Soviet television viewers— the videotape having been acquired from goodness knows where, although one can easily guess where and by whom.

What's more, certain experts had edited the videotape, where necessary, by slowing down the image for fractions of a second and by slowing down my words as I spoke them. I was told this by the television engineers at the Ostankino studios, who also wrote a letter to the commission that was set up to investigate the biased presentation of my visit in the Soviet press. But of course no one was going to investigate the scandalous fact that the videotape had been doctored. The main objective had been achieved; perplexed people—although they were few—were already wondering aloud whether I might really have been drunk. I considered it inappropriate to explain and justify myself.

It was one more lesson for me. I could not relax or lower my guard for a moment when faced by this system that hated me, that dogged my every footstep and pounced on every movement I might make, be it skillful or clumsy. And if I had known that over there, on another continent, I was being watched when I was almost asleep on my feet, I wouldn't have . . . What wouldn't I have done? Not taken the tablet? No, I couldn't have survived without some sleep. Would I have canceled the meeting? That, too, was out of the question. Most likely I shouldn't have forced myself to take that trip at such a pace. I have taken note of that for the future.

Soon afterward, however, another episode occurred, which literally hit me much harder. Once again, it was an organized, premeditated, provocative act. After a meeting with some of my constituents, I was being driven to the village of Uspenskoye in the countryside outside Moscow, to see an old friend of mine from Sverdlovsk days, who had a dacha there. Not far from his house I dismissed the driver, as I almost always do, in order to walk the last few hundred yards. The car, a Volga, drove away. I began to cross a bridge. Suddenly another car appeared behind me—and I was in the river. I will not describe my emotions here, but what I went through in those few minutes is something I never want to experience again.

The water was terribly cold. I got cramps in my legs and was barely able to swim to the shore, although the distance was only a few hundred yards. As I climbed up onto the bank, I collapsed and lay on the ground for some time, recovering my senses. Then I got up, shivering in the brutal cold. I realized that I would never make it to my friend's house on my own, and I staggered to the nearby police station.

The police on duty recognized me immediately. They asked me no questions, for I immediately instructed them not to tell anyone about the incident. While I was drinking the tea that the police gave me, and while my clothes were drying out a little, I cursed whoever had done this to me—"How low can they sink?"—but I made no official statement. My wife and daughter came to fetch me, and as I was leaving I again asked the policeman to say nothing to anyone about what had happened.

Why did I do that? I foresaw the reaction of those people who have had great difficulty in tolerating the moral provocations directed against me and would be incapable of accepting calmly the news of a physical attack on me. Zelenograd, where the majority of the electronics factories supply the defense industry, and Sverdlovsk, where there are even more armaments factories, might have staged a protest strike. Indeed, half of Moscow might have downed its tools. And then, as a result of strikes in the defense industries, martial law would have been declared and a state of "perpetual and ideal" order would have begun. Thus, as a result of Yeltsin's giving way to a provocation, *perestroika* (of the wrong sort) might have been achieved in our country.

Of course, I may be wrong. It is possible that my principle of always telling the truth might not have let me down. For it was that which most surprised my constituents—the fact that I was hiding something, not telling the whole story.

I still think that people will understand the incident and will work out the truth for themselves. Especially when Bakatin, the minister of internal affairs, reported at a session of the Supreme Soviet that no attempt had been made on my life, and as proof offered some false information. This made me even more certain that people would guess at the truth. For some reason, Bakatin even misled his listeners over facts that can easily be checked. He said, for instance, that if the victim of an attack really had been knocked off the bridge, he would have been seriously injured, because the bridge is fifty feet above the water. In fact, the distance from the bridge to the water is fifteen feet. So to make Bakatin's statement plausible, they should hastily build a new bridge—thirty-five feet higher than the previous one! But that would be too much, even to discredit Yeltsin.

Altogether I was certain that people would sense the numerous absurdities and inconsistencies in the version provided by the minister of internal affairs and would realize that something really had happened to me; and that they would understand the most important point of all: the reason why he had announced to the Supreme Soviet that there had been no attempt on my life.

The provocation did have some success at the time. My supporters announced in a panic that my popularity had fallen. Immediately a false rumor was sown in the soil prepared for it: that I had been going to see my mistress at her dacha, and she had for some reason thrown a bucketful of water over me! Although this is obvious nonsense, clearly the more improbable the concoction, the more likely it is to be believed. Moreover, people like hearing stories about the indiscretions of politicians.

Even so, I reacted calmly to what sociologists would call a drop in my ratings. I remain convinced that everything will fall into place and that this stupid and pointless story will not for long undermine the confidence of those people who have suddenly been given cause to doubt me. After all, in the end people are judged by real achievements and concrete results and not by myths and rumors.

After my involuntary bath in that ice-cold water, I was

seriously ill for two weeks, with a touch of pneumonia. For that reason, I watched part of the session of the Supreme Soviet on television. It turned out to be a very sorry spectacle, especially when one knew how serious the situation in the country was and how urgent it was to make certain decisions, since there was still a small chance that they might pull us out of a crisis. But those decisions were not being made; the enactment of essential new laws was put off to the indefinite future, and we were clearly slithering downhill to the point where not even the boldest and most progressive legislation could save us.

I remember Yuri Afanasiev, at the first session of the Congress of People's Deputies, graphically describing the newly elected Supreme Soviet as being "Stalinist-Brezhnevite" in makeup. For all my respect for the coiner of this phrase, I cannot agree with his assessment. Our Supreme Soviet is not "Stalinist-Brezhnevite"—that is if anything too high, or perhaps too low, an evaluation of it. It is "Gorbachevian," faithfully reflecting our chairman's inconsistency and timidity, his love of half-measures and semidecisions. Everything the Supreme Soviet does is undertaken too late. Like our chairman, it is constantly lagging behind the march of events. And that is why so many urgently needed measures have not been passed into law.

On the eve of the autumn 1989 session, as though to teach us a lesson, the totalitarian socialism forced on them by Stalin after the war collapsed in three of the socialist countries. And almost in mockery of our painful efforts at *perestroika* over more than four years, in a matter of days the German Democratic Republic, Czechoslovakia, Bulgaria, and now Rumania, have made the leap out of the past toward a normal, human, civilized society. It is not clear whether we shall ever be able to catch up to them. The opening of the Berlin Wall; new rules of entry and exit; new laws concerning the press and social organizations; the annulment of the articles in their constitutions guaranteeing the "leading role" of the Communist Party; the resignation of the central committees; the summoning of extraordinary party congresses; the condemnation of the invasion of Czechoslovakia—all this should have happened in our country four years ago. Instead, we have been marking time, terrified of taking a step forward and thereby jumping two steps back.

I am very glad that these changes have taken place in the neighboring socialist countries—glad for their sakes. But I also think that these changes will force us to think again and reassess what we so proudly call *perestroika*, and that we shall soon realize that we are practically the only country left on earth which is trying to enter the twenty-first century with an obsolete nineteenth-century ideology; that we are the last inhabitants of a country defeated by socialism, as one clever man put it.

The latest news: Rumors are going around Moscow that a coup is being planned for the next plenum of the Central Committee, with the aim of dismissing Gorbachev from his post of general secretary of the Central Committee of the Communist Party of the Soviet Union but leaving him as chairman of the Congress of People's Deputies. I don't believe these rumors, but even if they come true I shall fight for Gorbachev at the plenum. Yes, I shall fight for him—my perpetual opponent, the lover of half-measures and halfsteps. These tactics he prefers will eventually be his downfall; unless, of course, he realizes his chief failing in time. But for the present, at least until the next Party Congress, at which new leaders may emerge, he is the only man who can stop the ultimate collapse of the party.

Our right-wingers, unfortunately, fail to understand this. They believe that by the old mechanical method of voting by a show of hands they will succeed in turning back the clock of history.

The fact that these rumors circulate is, of course, symptomatic. Our huge country is balanced on a razor's edge, and nobody knows what will happen to it tomorrow.

It is slightly easier for the readers of this book than for me as I write. They will already know what has happened tomorrow, will know where I am and what has become of me.

They will already know what has happened to the Soviet Union. And to all of us.